THE CHRONICLES OF
BOOGIEFACE &
THE ANIMAL

THE CHRONICLES OF BOOGIEFACE & THE ANIMAL

One Small-Town Dad's Adventures in Fatherhood

VALENTINE J. BRKICH

Copyright © 2018 Valentine J. Brkich

All rights reserved. This book or any portion thereof may not be reproduced or used in any manner whatsoever without the express written permission of the publisher except for the use of brief quotations in a book review.

Bridge Street Books
P.O. Box 112
Beaver, PA 15009

ISBN-13: 978-0-9816877-5-9

Library of Congress Control Number: 2018903474

This book is dedicated to my wife, Cassie, for giving me two beautiful children, and to my children, for teaching me so much about life and love (and for giving me plenty of writing material).

Special thanks to my friend and mentor, James A. Perkins, for pushing me to make this book a reality.

Never raise your hand to your kids.
It leaves your groin unprotected.
— *Red Buttons*

Introduction

When I found out that my wife was pregnant with our first child, I was thrilled. And terrified. In that one moment everything changed, and I began to look at the world differently. It wasn't just about me anymore. Now I had a family to think about. This little baby was counting on me, and I wasn't about to let him or her down.

At least…that was the plan.

Immediately I began reading up on parenting. I went out and got all the best books on the subject and read them cover to cover. By the time my daughter was born, I was an expert on childbirth and parenting.

Yeah, right.

Sure, those books taught me the basics of parenting, like how to change a diaper (very carefully), and when to feed your baby (when she's screaming her head off), and so forth. But none of them could prepare me for the lack of sleep, the marathon bowel-movement sessions (theirs, not mine), the shattered oven doors, the inexplicable mood swings, the leaky diapers, the dinnertime battles, the inescapable clutter, and all the other things that make parenting one of the toughest jobs in the world (the others being coal mining and crocodile dentistry).

The following is a collection of stories I published on my blog—SmallTownDad.com—chronicling my first 10 years of fatherhood. They are stories of love and laughter. They are also stories of physical and mental exhaustion. For those of you who already have kids, I hope that these tales will bring you a laugh or two as you relate them to your own parenting experiences. For those of you who have yet to embark on the journey of parenthood, I hope they won't make you run for the hills.

I wrote these stories so that I would never forget the little things that make parenthood one of the most amazing and rewarding experiences a person can have. Furthermore, I wanted to make sure I had a written record of it all to share with my grown children one day, so they could see all the crap they put us through.

And, oh yeah, to show them how much joy they've brought into our lives. Enjoy.

Countdown to Fatherhood

Well, it's official. The final countdown has begun. My wife just entered her third trimester of pregnancy, which means I only have three more months of somewhat acceptable irresponsibility. After our first child is born, the stupid little things I usually do will cease to be cute and will suddenly become moronic.

For instance, last week I left the outside faucet on. As a result my new garden hose burst from the pressure, spraying water everywhere for about 20 minutes before I discovered it. By then the water had leaked into my basement and left a large puddle in the middle of the floor. I did this not once, mind you, but twice in two weeks, ruining two completely good hoses and bruising my fragile male ego in the process. My wife, although somewhat annoyed with my absentmindedness, was amused by my inexplicable yet endearing dopiness.

Fast forward to this fall when our house will be filled with binkies, Boppys®, Bumbos and all things baby. I can tell you right now that my innate dopiness will no longer be acceptable. Breaking a couple garden hoses is one thing; breaking a newborn baby is a completely different story. You can't just go to the local hardware store and pick up another one.

"Ah...yes, I need some 3/4-inch screws, a couple washers, and a new baby, please."

When I'm a daddy, I'll really have to be on my game. I'm actually going to have to think about every decision I make before I make it. This is a lot of pressure for someone who's basically been winging it for the past 30 years.

And if *I'm* nervous about all this, imagine how my wife must feel!

How is she supposed to trust giving a baby to someone who, on a daily basis, trips and falls going *up* the stairs?

My father-in-law has told me many, many times about the time when he and his friend were watching the kids while the women were out shopping. When the women returned just two short hours later, they found the men drinking beer and the two infants still in the playpen, right where they had left them. Only now the kids' diapers were dangerously close to bursting. I have to admit, at first I didn't see the big deal in all this. But then my wife explained how a playpen and a babysitter are actually two completely different things. Who knew?

This is how men think. It's frightening but true.

So I guess I only have a couple of months to get my act together and become a responsible, selfless caregiver. If all else fails, I'll just consider my first instinct and then do the exact opposite.

It should work like a charm.

The Baby Registry

When I last left you, my wife had just entered her third trimester of pregnancy. That puts us at just about two months until The Big Day. There have been some noticeable physical changes in both my wife and me over this past month. She continues to grow more beautiful with each passing day; I, on the other hand, continue to grow more panicked and frazzled.

Recently, we went to the local baby-stuff superstore to complete our baby registry. Five years ago before our wedding, we had a great time running around the department store zapping our favorite housewares with those super-cool, bar-code-reader-gun-thingies that they give you. I figured the baby registry would be just as fun.

I was mistaken.

Don't get me wrong, I was excited to pick out all the cute stuff we'll need for our little bundle of joy; I was just unprepared for the massive amount of equipment that's necessary to raise a baby nowadays. Columbus required fewer supplies when he sailed for the New World.

For all you guys out there, if you've never stepped inside one of these baby superstores, you're in for a real treat. It's like shopping on Mars. Imagine entering a store filled with thousands of items, all of which are completely foreign to you. (Much like when I go to the hardware store.) It's really hard to prepare yourself for this experience. Also, you may want to wear sunglasses in order to shade your eyes from the primary color onslaught as you enter the store. It's like a Crayola bomb exploded.

Everywhere you look, shell-shocked men push shopping carts aimlessly around the aisles, looking forlorn, the ghosts of long-lost frat parties haunting their every step. Meanwhile, their wives debate about whether to get the mauve breast milk tote or the sage one.

At one point we were confronted by Mr. Stroller Guy who, sounding much like a used-car salesman, showed us the various strollers and their features. As he rambled on about shocks, wheel-base and horsepower, I noticed other strollers made by Eddie Bauer and Jeep. I assume these are for when you get the urge to take your newborn baby on a jungle safari.

Now that our registry is complete, my father-in-law and I have to build a nursery so we'll have somewhere to put all this crap. He's hoping to create a cozy little nest for his newest grandchild; I'm just hoping I don't maim myself in the process.

Wish me luck.

Life On 24-Hour Baby Watch

We're in the final days now. My wife and I have made it through 38 long weeks of pregnancy, and they tell us it can happen any time now. It's like I'm an inmate on Baby Row, and there's no chance the governor will call to commute my sentence. I have nothing to do now but sit and wait for the inevitable.

Over the past few weeks we've been making all the necessary preparations for our new roommate. I've been putting the finishing touches on the nursery, while Cassie's been putting together our Hospital Supply Kit, which is comprised of a suitcase filled with clothing and toiletries, a backpack filled with various games and reading materials, and a small cooler to be packed with ice chips and energy drinks. All of these have been strategically placed in the living room where they can be picked up and loaded into the car in a minute's notice. It's kind of like we're packing for vacation, only this time we'll be bringing back a brand-new human being instead of a box of saltwater taffy.

Over the past several weeks we've also been attending a weekly labor-and-delivery class so that we'll know what to expect when the time comes. This is where I got to see my first childbirth video. If you've never had the pleasure, lucky you. The hardest part was sitting there with the teacher and the other couples, while I pretended like what I was watching was no big deal. On the outside I'm watching "Bambi"; on the inside I'm watching "Aliens." In 3D. Fortunately it was a baby that emerged from the pregnant woman and not some bloodthirsty space creature with razor-sharp teeth and acid for blood.

Throughout this time of preparation, my wife and I have been gathering dozens of baby-related gifts from our friends and relatives. Our house is now an obstacle course of car seats, bassinets, diapers, baby toys, baby clothes, and other random piles of infant-related, Chinese-made, hopefully-not-lead-based-painted items. Right now, as I'm sitting in my office, I'm looking at a Diaper Champ, a Bumbo (whatever the heck that is) and a portable stroller called an "umbrella chair," which, strangely enough, provides no protection from the rain. Right before my eyes my office is slowly morphing into a Babies "R" Us.

The next time you hear from me I'll be a father. (Frightening, isn't it?) Hopefully, after this life-changing experience, I'll still manage to hang onto my dry wit and sarcasm, but I'm not making any promises. I'm told that a new baby "changes everything." And from the looks of my office, I'm starting to believe it.

Let's just hope I don't confuse my paper shredder for the diaper can. That would be ugly.

Welcome to Fatherhood—Beware of the Purple Slime

For months now my wife and I have been making preparations for the arrival of our first child. We've read all the best books on pregnancy and natural childbirth; we've watched videos and listened to experts; we've even practiced relaxation techniques, all so that, when the moment finally arrived, we'd be ready.

How naïve of us.

Nothing can prepare you for childbirth. No book, no class, no shockingly revealing video. And no one ever told me about the purple slime, either.

Cassie went into labor at 1:30 a.m. on her actual due date. At first, since her contractions were mild, she allowed me to continue to sleep so that I could save up my energy. You see, I was the "coach," and it would be my job to support her throughout the process. We would soon discover, however, that my coaching skills would amount to diddly squat once the real fun began. Then I would change from coach to horrified spectator.

By 6:30 a.m. the contractions had become much stronger and closer together, so we packed up the S.U.V. and took off for the hospital. At this time my wife was in major discomfort, but nothing she couldn't handle. This was going to be a piece of cake. After all, we had read a lot of books.

By 8 a.m. Cass was 6-7 cm dilated and progressing rapidly. Apparently we had purchased the Express Delivery Package. This is when the contractions ceased being mildly uncomfortable and became mildly excruciating. I could tell this by my wife's bone-crushing grasp of my hand, her bloodcurdling screams, and the fact that her eyeballs were now protruding from their sockets. For a moment I questioned the decision not to use drugs. But if she could do it, so could I.

By 9 a.m. my wife was fully dilated, i.e., she wanted me dead. It was at this time when I sensed she was ready to push. I knew this because I had read a lot about the delivery process, and also because she kept screaming, "I FEEL LIKE I HAVE TO PUSH!" Moments later the doctor entered the room, looked down at my wife, and in a very nonchalant way said, "Oh look, there's the head." Two pushes later and my daughter's head—all purple and slimy—popped out into the world. Fortunately her body followed shortly thereafter.

It was the most amazing experience of my life. Finally, after months and months of waiting, here was our new baby girl. She was the most beautiful thing I had ever seen, purple slime and all.

Now we enter the new and exciting world of parenthood—a world of poopie diapers, disappearing binkies and long, sleepless nights. Some would say the hard part is just beginning. But I'm not worried.

Remember, I've read a lot of books.

Great Sleeps of the Past

Some people fantasize about hitting it rich. Others, about being famous, falling in love, or going on a trip to some exotic, far-off destination. I fantasize about sleep—long, restful, uninterrupted sleep.

Since my daughter was born last month, the longest I've slept in one continuous stretch is two and a half, maybe three hours, max. Sometimes it's even less than that. Have you ever tried to function on two hours' sleep? Your brain knows it needs more sleep and, therefore, it rebels against you, making it difficult to perform even the simplest of tasks, such as dressing yourself or remembering your wife's name.

Recently I've found myself recalling great sleeps of my past. I didn't even know it was possible to remember a particular *sleep* before my baby was born. Now these vivid memories of slumber are coming back to me in waves.

For example, the other night I was rocking my daughter while watching TV, when something sparked an old childhood memory. One time when I was at my friend's house during the winter, we were supposed to sleep on the pullout couch in the living room. It was cold that night, however, and we decided it would be much more comfortable to sleep in the heated twin water beds up in his bedroom. So we went upstairs, kicked his little brother out, and then enjoyed a blissful night's sleep, each of us snug in our very own heated water bed.

That was twenty-some years ago, and I had never really given much thought to it since. But this is the kind of stuff you daydream about when you're a new parent—prolonged, satisfying, uninterrupted sleep. As I sat there holding my daughter the other night, I swear I could almost feel the comforting warmth of that water bed, and it brought a smile to my face.

Just then my daughter projectile-vomited in my eye.

My older sister has two kids. As she held my daughter for the first time, she said that she "didn't remember her kids ever being so tiny." It wasn't the first time I've heard a parent say this. Now I understand that the reason you don't remember things about these earlier times is because, due to extreme sleep deprivation, your brain was only functioning at maybe 25-percent capacity, and your long-term memory was temporarily shut down altogether. Basically, you were a zombie.

I'd love to be able share more great sleeps stories with you; however, my daughter just dozed off and they say that when your baby sleeps, you should try to do the same. So if you'll excuse me, I think I'll just…*zzzzzzzzzzzzzz.*

NEWSFLASH: A Baby Changes Everything!

Whenever you have a baby, you are bombarded with advice from other parents. Apparently all you have to do to become an expert on childrearing is to have a child.

There's one particular piece of advice that you receive so much during the first few weeks, it's enough to make you sick: "A baby changes everything." It comes at you from every direction. You can't avoid it. Other parents seem fiendishly happy to impart this sage advice on you, as if they're the first to break it to you that you having a baby may alter your life a little.

Thanks for the tip.

What's funny is how each parent that tells you this seems to think that they're dropping some sort of information bombshell on you. Like you have no clue that introducing a fragile, 100-percent dependent, 24-hour-a-day, crying-and-pooping machine into your life just may put a slight damper on your current lifestyle.

One of the more notable changes, at least in my house, has been with my ability to move around freely. Before the baby, I'd stomp around my house whenever and wherever I wanted without ever thinking about the sound my steps were making. Now I can tell you exactly where every creaky floorboard is and the particular path you must take in order to avoid it.

You see, when you have a baby and you somehow manage to get it to fall asleep, it's like a magic trick. Once you've accomplished this incredible feat, you'll do anything to keep that baby asleep for as long as possible, just so you can get a few things done. If this means tiptoeing through your house as if it were a minefield, so be it.

Our house has some creaky hardwood floors. So if I have to get past my baby while she's napping in her crib, I must become a ninja. One misstep and she could wake up, effectively ending another brief moment of freedom. A couple times, after putting her down for a nap, I've actually crawled out of the room, hugging the ground like a Special Forces commando.

Of course, this is just one of the many changes you experience with a baby in the house. I refuse, however, to be like everyone else and say that *everything* changes. Once you become comfortable being a parent and your baby develops a sleeping schedule, I'm sure your life returns somewhat back to normal.

Doesn't it?

Six Months In—So Far, So Good

Some companies put you on a six-month probationary period when they hire you, just to make sure you're the right person for the job. Recently, my wife and I hit the six-month mark as first-time parents. It's been a real challenge at times, but I think we've passed the test, thus far. Hopefully my daughter will decide to keep us.

I thought it would be interesting to look back and review the changes that have occurred over the last half year. First, let's review my daughter's progress:

- In her first six months of life, Boogieface, as I now call her, thanks to her perpetually runny nose, nearly doubled in weight. They tell me this is a good thing. I just hope, for her sake, that this trend doesn't continue for the rest of her life.

- She also has less hair now than she did when she was born, with hardly anything on the sides, and the bulk of it being on the top of her head. Think George McFly in a diaper.

- She now sleeps through the night consistently, unlike the first few months when a two-hour stretch was a treat. We refer to that time as "The Zombie Days."

- And finally, she can now hold her head up under her own power and, with every passing day, looks less and less like a bobble-head.

Now let's review the changes in Mommy and Daddy over the past six months:

- We no longer go running to the nursery at the slightest noise or cry. Now, we just turn off the baby monitor altogether. We get more sleep that way.
- It now takes me less than 30 seconds to change a diaper. If baby-diapering was an Olympic event, I'd be on a box of Wheaties.
- Our sleeping time has increased and, consequently, our brains are almost fully functional again. Which is nice.
- I have almost completely overcome my fear of bodily fluids.
- Finally, I've given up on having a clean house ever again. It's just not going to happen.

So, there you have it – my official parenthood six-month report. I'd give us a B+ grade so far, with an A for effort. Heck, the hard part's over. It has to get easier from here on out. Right?

Welcome Changes

Recently, Boogieface began speaking. I think her exact words were "Bwha, bwha, bwha, bwha...sppppppuffffffff!" It's not exactly the Gettysburg Address, but if you ask me it's pretty impressive for someone who's never even heard of the alphabet.

I try to communicate with her by imitating her unique language, but she usually just stares back at me with that Do-I-know-you? look on her face. It's funny, but I'm never embarrassed about how I sound when I'm "talking" with my baby in her strange infant tongue. Strangers can be watching and I'll still babble incoherently and make clownish faces, all without a trace of self-consciousness. But of course that's what happens when you become a parent; you lose every last ounce of self-respect.

It's amazing how much you really do change when you become a parent. For example, often when I'm changing her diaper, my daughter will pee on my hands. In years past, if anyone would've peed on my hands, I would've sprinted to the nearest sink and scrubbed them raw. Now they get peed on all the time and, amazingly, it doesn't bother me, as long as it's my daughter who's doing the peeing.

Lately, we discovered that we can make her smile just by looking at her and going "buh, buh, buh, buh, buh." Don't ask me how we figured this out. Now we're constantly buh-buh-buh-ing wherever we go, and we couldn't care less who sees us. We've completely lost our minds.

Becoming a father has changed me in some positive ways, too. For one, I'm much more patient now. When Boogs wakes up and realizes she's lost her pacifier or "binky" (technical term), she does what she does best: she cries. And so, either I or my wife (usually my wife) will get out of bed, stumble to the nursery, and re-insert said binky into the baby's mouth. Sometimes this does the trick. Sometimes, however, after just a few seconds, she spits the binky out again, which in turn triggers the crying. Then, it's my turn to do the zombie walk back to the nursery and re-insert said binky. This cycle continues until Boogieface asleep or until her crying escalates to blood-curdling screaming.

A couple times I was so desperate I actually considered attaching the binky to her face. Unfortunately, you can never find the duct tape when you really need it.

Yes, when you become a parent, change is inevitable. You just have to be able to roll with the punches. Bend, don't break, as they say.

Or as Boogieface says, "Bwha, bwha…spppppppuffffffff."

Warning: Your Baby May Be
Hazardous to Your Health

So, the other day I'm walking down Third Street with my wife and our baby girl. It's a beautiful spring day, the sun is out, and I feel energized after what has been a long winter indoors.

My wife is pushing the baby in the stroller. I am walking alongside, just ahead of the stroller. Of course, as we walk, I'm also making goofy, embarrassing faces at her (the baby, not my wife). I do this because it makes her smile, and nothing makes me happier than seeing that big, toothless grin.

And then I walk straight into an iron railing.

Somehow, while making silly faces at my daughter, I fail to notice a handicap-entrance ramp and its accompanying metal railing. The top part of the railing hits me right in the sternum, and the lower part makes direct, forceful contact with the soft part of my right knee. Thankfully, there is no contact with the middle part of the railing, if you catch my drift. The collision stops me dead in my tracks. A moment later I'm hopping around in agony as my wife laughs uncontrollably. Boogs, meanwhile, is giving me one of those Are-you-really-my-daddy? looks.

I'm a clumsy person as it is. Throw an adorable little baby into the mix, and you've got a recipe for disaster. She's so darn cute, I can't take my eyes off of her. This can be dangerous (as we have seen) when doing things where forward vision is imperative, such as walking towards an iron railing.

The Land of Fatherhood is beset with peril. Take the dreaded Pee Attack, for example, which can strike at any moment. One minute you're changing a diaper, the next you're dodging a fountain-like spray of fresh, warm urine. Meanwhile, your baby just lies there, blissfully unapologetic.

Other times, your baby will use her innate cuteness to manipulate you into losing your inhibitions. Suddenly you're making silly faces and babbling sounds in public places like restaurants, grocery stores, or the DMV, completely unaware that you're being watched. By the time you come to your senses, it's too late, and humiliation sets in.

These are just some of the hazards that come with being a dad. Some lead to physical injury; others can leave you mentally scarred and publicly disgraced. And this is just in the first few months.

Who knows what terrors lay ahead in the teenage years? (Heaven help me.)

Bruised sternums and egos aside, these hazards are a small price to pay for the immeasurable joy your baby brings you. Just watch out for the pee. It really stings the eyes.

Germ Warfare

I never used to get sick. My immune system was hardened years ago in my college fraternity house, where raccoons prowled the chapter room, the floor was an ashtray, and bathrooms were cleaned monthly, if at all. By the time I graduated, my body, coated by a thick inner lining of Milwaukee's Best Light and Jose Cuervo residue, was impervious to even the most aggressive of germs.

Since leaving that germ-ridden environment, my defenses have weakened considerably. And now that I'm a father, I know that it will only get worse. You see, kids are like germ magnets, and once they attract the germs, they inevitably pass them on to you.

Every since my niece has been going to preschool, my parents, who watch her during the day, are constantly fighting some type of malady, from the sniffles to full-blown influenza. And there's not much they can do about it. My niece brings the germs home and, in no time at all, my parents are coughing and sneezing and doing shots of NyQuil. This is, after all, how the Black Plague began back in the 14th century. The "experts" will tell you that rats were responsible for spreading the disease, but actually it was just some kid who forgot to wash his hands at school.

Recently, after a family gathering, Boogieface fell ill and expelled her recently eaten prunes all over our once white carpet. The minute everything was cleaned up, she followed with an encore performance and later soiled both her pajamas and bedding while sleeping in her crib. The smell is permanently burnt into my nasal cavity.

Two days later, she was fine but my wife was deathly ill. So much so that we had to take her to the emergency room in the middle of the night to get treated for severe dehydration. As I coated everything in the house with a thick layer of Lysol, I hoped and prayed that I would be spared the same fate.

I wasn't.

The next morning I nearly passed out en route to the bathroom, where I remained on the floor for several moments, my head resting against the cool, merciful porcelain, until I could drag my aching, feverish body over to the couch. There I remained for two days, paralyzed and tortured by some type of merciless, evil, super-flu on steroids.

I'm happy to report that my wife, daughter, and I are all now fully recovered. However, we both realize our days of perfect health are over. The more gatherings we attend, the more our little girl will be passed around from person to person, picking up all types of head colds, chest colds, stomach flus, 24-hour flus, rhinoviruses, noroviruses, sore throats, strep throats, sinus infections, respiratory infections, and so on, which she will then, of course, pass on to us.

It's just another one of the perks of parenthood.

Gentlemen, Start Your Babies!

So, here we go. Time to enter the next phase of parenthood: The Mobile Years.

Up until now, things have been pretty simple. Sure, the past 10 and a half months have certainly been challenging with the midnight feedings, diaper disasters, missing binkies, etc. But until just the other day, our baby girl had been pretty much sedentary. This was one of our favorite things about her. She could roll around a little, but basically wherever you left her is where she'd be when you returned. Not anymore.

The other day Boogieface figured out how to crawl. Granted, she's not breaking any land-speed records just yet. But she's moving, nonetheless. Farewell to those lazy days of lying on the floor watching our cute little stationary baby do cute little stationary baby things. Welcome to the days of endlessly chasing after her, saying "No!" and "Don't touch that!" and "Hey, drop that beer!"

There is so much more to worry about now. When a baby is just a few months old, you can basically set her anywhere and be confident that she'll still be there whenever you get back. For example, after giving her a bath in the sink, you can leave her on the kitchen counter while you run off to grab a towel from the bathroom, knowing that she'll be right where you left her when you return. Not that I would ever do such a thing.

But now this has all changed. Now we have to keep an eye on her at all times. Now we have to "baby-proof" the house, as they say. We have to scan every inch of it for anything she might grab and choke on or pull over or break. We have to cordon off certain areas of our house with those annoying and unsightly baby gates. We have to understand that, if we set her down somewhere, say in the living room, whilst we run off to check our email, there's a good chance she won't be in the living room when we get back. Again, not that I've ever done that.

The one thing I really don't want to do is put those ugly little rubber guards over all the sharp corners on our furniture. Maybe we could just sell our dangerous wooden furniture and replace it with more baby-friendly inflatable furniture. Do they make inflatable coffee tables?

There are some good things, however, about my daughter being able to crawl. For one, now she can go get her own toy instead of making Daddy, who's had a long day at work, get up off the couch and get it for her. Plus, if I wanted to, I could sit on the couch and toss things across the room for her to go fetch, sort of like if we had a new puppy.

Not that I would ever do such a thing.

Daddy Delusions

Attention, all guys! Want to know what it's like to be famous? Do you want to know what it feels like to turn heads when you walk into a room? Would you like to experience the same admiration enjoyed by big-name celebs like Brad Pitt, Matthew McConaughey, and Leonardo DiCaprio? Then just strap a baby to your chest. (Preferably, your own baby.)

Just recently, my wife and I took in one of Western PA's many fine autumn festivals. Our baby girl isn't much for strollers, so we bought one of those Swedish, yuppie front-side baby carrier thingies. Boogieface loves it. She kicks her feet and waves her hands as she bounces up and down with my every step. We sort of look like Siamese twins, except that we don't look very much alike, and I'm a few decades older.

During the festival, nearly every person we passed was oohing and aahing at our little diaper diva, commenting on her cuteness, pointing her out to friends and relatives and – I'll admit it – making Daddy feel very much like a celebrity.

Now, I know what you're thinking. They weren't fawning over you, you idiot. Obviously I know this. I may be somewhat dopey and unable to do simple math, but I am able to grasp the fact that these people are taken by my daughter and not by me.

So what's so wrong about pretending? It's not as if I'm some overbearing "stage dad," parading my daughter in a baby beauty pageant or forcing her to practice golf so that she'll be the next Tiger (or Tigress) Woods. I'm just strapping her to my chest and frequenting public festivals so that I can pretend that the attention she's getting is actually for me and my striking good looks.

And trust me, fellas, nothing draws attention, specifically female attention, better than an adorable little baby. A lot of people will try to tell you that a puppy works just as well, but I disagree. Just try putting a dog in a front-side carrier and watch the looks that people give you. Besides, every time you walk past a tree the dog pees all over you. Been there, done that.

If only I had known all this back when I was single. Back then, girls avoided looking at me as if I were a solar eclipse, Medusa, or the Elephant Man. Little did I know that all I had to do was strap a baby to my chest and I'd be the toast of the town.

As we were leaving the festival, my wife and I passed a young couple going the other way. The guy was one of those big, burly football-player types. As they passed us, I heard the girl giggle and ask her boyfriend if he could ever see himself wearing a baby on his chest. I turned back and caught him looking back at me. I smiled, and he gave me a look that said "Dork."

That's OK, Big Burly Football-Player Guy. Laugh now, but remember: I was once just like you (only much skinnier and awkward, and sans girlfriend). Don't be surprised if, one day, you find yourself wearing a baby on your chest and soaking up the attention from every female in sight.

There are worse ways to spend the afternoon.

Problem Child

I have a confession to make, and I'm a little embarrassed about it. Actually, it's not even about me. It's about my daughter. She has a problem. A few, actually. And I think that, although she'll probably be upset with me, the best way to deal with these problems is to talk about them openly and honestly and reveal them to a bunch of total strangers.

First of all – and there's really no easy way to say this – my daughter pees herself. All the time. She goes No. 2 in her pants all the time, too. It's a daily occurrence, several times a day, actually. It's so bad that she has to wear a diaper all the time, even when she sleeps. We've tried to tell her that she needs to use the toilet, but she just looks at us and babbles incoherently. It's like she doesn't even know what a toilet is.

And that's another problem: communication. When my wife and I want something, we just ask for it. But my daughter is stubborn, and she never tells us exactly what it is she wants. Instead, she just cries or screams or throws things forcing us to guess. When she does this at home, it's aggravating; when we're in public, it's mortifying. People just stare at us like we're crazy.

I'm also sorry to say that my daughter has a drinking problem. You should see her. She can never take a drink without spilling it all over herself, and sometimes she even misses her mouth completely. They say the first step to recovery is admitting you have a problem in the first place. But we can't even get her to say "mama"— how in the world are we supposed to get her to say "I have a drinking problem?"

Another thing is the way she eats. It's disgusting. She refuses to use utensils and eats everything with her bare hands. Half the time she misses her mouth completely, and the food ends up all over her face, her outfit, and all over the floor. And when she's had her fill, instead of just saying she's finished, she starts playing with her food and throwing it all over the place. It's a real problem.

One last thing (and this may be the most embarrassing of all), my daughter has a bad habit of chewing on *everything*. Rocks, sticks, other human beings, etc.—you name it, she'll stick it in her mouth and chew on it. The wooden frame of her bed has so many teeth marks on it, you'd think we're raising a beaver.

For now all we can do is hope that she'll grow out of all these bad habits and become a normal, respectable member of society. In the meantime, we'll just have to deal with her infantile behavior the best we can.

Now, if you'll excuse me, I think she's eating the remote control.

The Same Old Song and Dance

I fear sequins. I loathe the sound of taps on hardwood, and I despise French terms like plié, jeté, and échappé. You see, I have two sisters, both of whom were in dancing school before they could walk. And for several years, I was dragged along to suffer.

So you can see why when my daughter was born, one of my first edicts was that she would never taking dancing lessons. As far as I'm concerned, there are plenty of other physical activities to partake in – soccer, golf, curling, Jai alai, the biathlon – anything but dancing.

When I was a kid, every Wednesday as soon as my sisters and I got home from school, my mother would pack us into our International Scout and cart us off to dancing school, which was in a dusty old American Legion building. For the next couple hours or so I'd sit in the corner and write or draw while my sisters learned the basics of tap, jazz, and ballet. The Tyrannosauric commands of their dancing instructor still reverberate in my brain to this day.

Finally, my father would come and rescue me on his way home from work. From there we'd head to the bowling alley for his weekly league, and I'd sit in that smoky building for another hour or so, writing and drawing amidst the constant cursing and the incessant sound of urethane colliding with maple. Eventually, my mom and sisters would pick me up on their way home from dancing school. We did this every Wednesday for about 45 years or so.

And let's not forget the recitals: four or five mind-numbing hours of sequin-clad dancers performing routines set to some of the worst music ever written. To this day, just hearing a few notes of "The Heat is On" can throw me into a panic, as I relive the many dreadful hours I spent trapped in some dark high-school auditorium.

So you can see how when Boogieface began to show an inclination to dance, I became concerned. Ever since she's been able to stand on two feet, if music is playing, she's dancing. And the worst part is she's actually pretty good.

A couple weeks ago we were at street festival in town where some local dancing schools put on a show. Boogs was mesmerized by the performances and, to the delight of dozens of onlookers, mimicked every move with uncanny precision. She displayed rhythm, grace, coordination, and remarkable dancing ability. It was terrible!

Now everyone's telling me the same thing: "You *HAVE* to send that girl to dancing school. She's really talented!"

Oh joy.

If I'm doomed to spend the next 10 to 15 years of my life sitting through dancing lessons and recitals and listening to that horrid music. I just hope we've gotten past the Glenn Frey era. I don't know if I can handle it.

Man vs. Toddler: A Never-Ending Struggle

One of the first things you learn as a parent is that getting your child to listen to you is about as easy as teaching an elephant to do a cartwheel. Actually, it's much harder than that. Fortunately there are several things you can try in order to gain control over your offspring.

The first and by far the least effective method is simply asking your child to do whatever it is you want him or her to do. This one's a real roll of the dice. If you're lucky and your kid is too young to know better, you might actually get them to go to sleep just by asking them to. But more than likely, they'll decide pretty early on that you're an idiot and anything you want them to do can't possibly be right. That's just the way it is. It's God's little joke on us.

The second and much more effective way to get your kid to listen to you is through deception. It didn't take us long to realize that if we really wanted our daughter to do something, trickery was our only option.

Take eating, for example. Adults love to eat. We're addicted to it. Heck, entire industries have revolved around our inability to *stop* eating. Kids, on the other hand, could take it or leave it. If it wasn't for us adults constantly shoving food down their throats three times a day, kids would go for weeks without eating anything.

Boogieface started out as a good eater, but we now realize it was more of an innate reflex than a conscious decision. Now that she's a toddler, getting her to eat what we want, when we want, has forced us to become masters of deception. For a while, the best way to get her to eat something was to tell her not to eat it. "Don't you eat that broccoli!"

I'd say. "That's Daddy's broccoli!" As soon as I'd say this, she'd stuff a floret in her mouth and flash a fiendish grin, the little devil.

The effectiveness of this reverse psychology was fleeting, however, and soon we were looking for another solution. The answer was bribery. If you want your kid to do something, nothing works better than offering them something in return. And it doesn't even have to be something good.

For example, a toddler doesn't understand that a remote control with batteries is much more effective than one without batteries. They just want to hold a remote—any remote. So, if they're bogarting the remote control, just find another remote and make like it's the greatest thing in the world. (If you can't find another remote, just use something else like a spatula or a banana. Don't worry, they won't know.) When you do this, your kid will immediately drop the real remote like a hot potato and demand the one you're holding. Soon you'll be happily surfing the channels, and your kid will be off looking for something metal to stick in the electrical outlet.

So the lesson here is, if you want your kid to listen to you, lie to them. Sure, they may end up not trusting you later in life, but that's all right. The key is surviving these early years.

After that, you can just bribe them with money.

Speaking in Tongues

I've always wanted to speak a second language. I took three years of Spanish in high school and another in college. Yet, even with four years of instruction, I'm still limited to just a few phrases:

"Me llamo Val." (My name is Val)
"Donde esta la biblioteca?" (Where is the library?)
"Feliz Navidad!" (Merry Christmas!)

Unfortunately, these phrases aren't very useful unless I'm in Mexico (or Miami) on Christmas day, and I need something to read, which has only happened once or twice before.

Recently, I've been learning a brand new language: baby-talk. Over the past few months Boogieface has been gradually increasing her vocabulary, and, as a result, she is getting better at communicating her needs. When I say *vocabulary*, however, I'm not necessarily talking about actual English words as you and I know them. Hers is a hybrid language of sorts—one part English and one part jibberish.

Sometimes she's easy to understand. Words, like *eat* and *play*, come out clear and phonetically correct. Other words, however, are not so clear, and it took some time for us to be able to first identify and then translate them.

For example, "waah," as we have come to learn, means "rag," which is what my daughter calls the cloth diaper she sleeps with. And when she says "why," she's not asking a question, she's asking for "water." The confusion doesn't end there, either.

One of my daughter's unique linguistic traits is that she likes to add the "uh" sound before a lot of her words, while putting the emphasis on the latter half. For example: "uh-EAT", "uh-PLAY", "uh-POO-PEE", etc. Sometimes she even puts an "uh" sound at the end of the word, which makes her sound almost Italian, i.e., "uh-WOK-uh," meaning "Put me down; I want to walk." Here's a little sampling of some of her most common phrases and their corresponding meanings:

uh-MALK-uh = I want my milk.

uh-DUCK-uh = It is dark in here.

uh-MAN-uh = I want a banana.

uh-SEAT-uh = Sit down.

shoosh = shoes

moe = more

uh oh = I spilled something (usually on purpose)

aw doe! = Get me out of this highchair or I'll start throwing food all over the place!

Each night before bedtime, she quickly runs through several of these phrases in a last-ditch effort to avoid going to sleep. ("Uh-EAT! Uh-MALK-uh! Uh-PAY! Uh-EAT!!)

I used to listen to other babies babble and wonder at the ability of their parents to translate what they were saying. Now I have this same superpower, which is pretty cool. Unfortunately, I also now find myself speaking back to my daughter in a way that makes me sound a little like a caveman:

"Daddy love you!"

"Bad girl! You listen Daddy. Daddy mad!"

"Shhh! Mommy tired. Mommy sleep."

"No touch Daddy's wine—NO TOUCH!"

It's not so bad talking like this at home, but out in public it can be a little embarrassing. I just wonder how long I'll continue to speak like this. ("Daddy no like boyfriend. Boyfriend have mustache and tattoo. Where Daddy's wine?")

So maybe the four years I spent studying Spanish were all for naught. That's OK. It's not like all those years of studying advanced mathematics did me any good, either. I still need a calculator to figure out the tip. Besides, I can now count baby-talk as my official second language.

Although I'm not sure it does anything for my resume.

What a Difference Ten Years Makes

Over the past few weeks I've come to the conclusion that the me of just ten years ago would hate the me of today. In fact, I think that 24-Year-Old Me would absolutely loathe 34-Year-Old Me and what I've become.

This enlightenment came to me a couple weeks back when two of my best friends invited me to accompany them on a little snowboarding getaway to a local mountain resort. The plan was to head up there early on Saturday and snowboard most of the day, while stopping for several breaks at the ski lodge bar. It was a fantastic plan, filled with all kinds of winter fun with two of my closest compadres, and it was one that 24-Year-Old Me would have jumped on.

34-Year-Old Me, however, decided to forgo this day of winter revelry and instead spend the day at the children's museum with my wife and daughter. Whilst my friends were out shushing down some icy slope, stopping for the occasional drink and spying the occasional snow bunny, I was one of what seemed like a thousand parents crammed into the Mr. Rogers' Neighborhood room, chasing my little one around with a video camera. It was a wonderful afternoon that concluded with my exhausted but happy daughter passing out in her car seat on the ride home.

24-Year-Old Me is just sick hearing about this.

The funny thing is, although I knew my friends were out having a great time, I was really glad I decided not to go. I gave up a day of adrenaline-pumping outdoor excitement with two of my best buds in order to watch my daughter paint an unrecognizable blob and then try to eat the paintbrush—and I was OK with it.

Right now, 24-Year-Old Me wants to throw up.

What can I say? My priorities have changed. 24-Year-Old Me's priorities were 1) looking for girls, and 2) making enough money bussing tables to buy beer for the week. 34-Year-Old Me's priorities on the other hand are 1) spending time with my wife and daughter, and 2) making enough money to buy wine for the week.

24-Year-Old Me really hates that I like wine.

Here's what a typical conversation between 24-year-old me and 34-year-old me would sound like:

24-Year-Old Me: *Hey, you wanna go to happy hour after work on Friday and look for some girls?*

34-Year-Old Me: *That sounds fun, but I think I'm just going to stay home, play with my daughter until she goes to sleep, and then maybe have a glass of wine or two before turning in.*

24-Year-Old Me: *What?!? Wine?!? Turn in early?!? Didn't you hear me? I'm talking about girls and beer!*

34-Year-Old Me: *I heard you. I'd just rather spend a nice quiet evening at home with my wife and daughter. Did you know our daughter can already say her A-B-Cs? She's really into Elmo now, too.*

24-Year-Old Me: (blank stare) *Uh…yeah. You have fun sitting at home then. I'll be out having a great time and meeting a bunch of girls.*

34-Year-Old Me: *No you won't. You never had the guts to talk to any girls. Besides, you always felt like crap the next day from drinking too much cheap beer.*

24-Year-Old Me: *I don't know what you're talking about, Mr. Turn-in-early-wine-drinker.*

34-Year-Old Me: *Yeah, Whatever.*

24-Year-Old Me: *Whatever, yourself!!*

34-Year-Old Me: *Wait…aren't we the same person?*

24-Year-Old Me: *Huh?*

34-Year-Old Me: *Oh…never mind.*

Yes, I'm perfectly happy with 34-Year-Old Me. Sure, 24-Year-Old Me had a lot of spunk and was always up for a good time. But then again, 24-Year-Old Me didn't know what its like to have your baby girl sit on your lap and smile while you read her favorite bedtime story. Too bad. I think 24-Year-Old Me might have really liked it.
24-Year-Old Me me seriously doubts that.

I Need a Timeout

The lines have been drawn. The battle has begun. After almost two years of peaceful coexistence, my daughter and I are now entrenched in a war of wills. We have officially entered that challenging phase of parenthood known as The Terrible Twos (*insert scary "Da, da, daaaa!" sound*).

Before I was a father, I hated when parents would talk about this infamous period of childhood development. I heard horror stories of inconsolable, uncontrollable toddlers causing public scenes and wreaking Godzilla-like havoc. I used to scoff at such tales. How could someone so young and so small possibly cause so much trouble? It must be bad parenting, I thought. Certainly, when my time came, I would fare better.

How foolish of me.

In her brief time here on Earth, my daughter has seemed somewhat advanced for her age. So it's no surprise that her Terrible Twos started right around 18 months. Our sweet little angel – always well behaved, always a good eater – suddenly decided one day that she wasn't going to listen to us anymore, and that food wasn't something you put in your mouth but rather something you threw across the room. It was if one morning we woke up and our daughter's angel wings had been replaced with devilish horns.

Back in the old days, the remedy for such behavior would've been a firm spanking with a custom-made wooden paddle (preferably one with copious holes drilled through it for added velocity). My wife and I, however, do not subscribe to this type of punishment. Instead, we put our faith in a kinder, gentler form of discipline, the Timeout, which we believe is a much more effective and humane method.

Besides, we've seen it work on TV.

The first couple times we put Boogieface in Timeout, it worked perfectly. Sitting alone on the special Timeout Chair in the Timeout Corner, she wailed in shame and shed rivers of tears as she begged for our forgiveness. Then, after letting her think about it for a minute or so, we'd ask for an apology and give her a hug as she whimpered in defeat. That'll teach her to fling mashed potatoes across the room!

It wasn't long, however, before she lost her fear of this trendy form of punishment. Now the once dreaded Timeout is about as threatening as a toothless chihuahua. "Do you want to go in Timeout!?", I say in my best angry-parent voice. "Yes!", she answers, nodding and flashing a fiendish smile.

Funny. This never happened on TV.

Maybe the Terrible Twos isn't caused by bad parenting after all. Maybe it's just a natural part of the development process. Then again, maybe it's God's way of having a good laugh at our expense.

Personally, I don't know how much more I can take. It's exhausting. Maybe I'll just put myself in Timeout for a while and think about it.

Jumpy-Things and Giant Thing-A-Ma-Jiggers

As winter fast approaches and we're beginning to spend more time indoors, I can already sense the first tinglings of cabin fever. Unfortunately, in my area when the weather's bad, there aren't many options for indoor family fun other than the library or the mall. Don't get me wrong, I love the library. It's free, it's close by, and there are plenty of books to keep my little one occupied. However, it also requires you to be quiet – an alien concept for a two-year-old brain.

At the local mall, on the other hand, you can be as loud as you want, and there's plenty of room for a toddler to run around and burn-off some energy. Then again, the hard tile flooring isn't the ideal surface for a child like mine, who likes to use her face to break her fall.

Searching online for something a little more toddler-friendly, Cass came across one of those family fun complexes with everything from mini-golf to arcade games. Most important, they had one of those big inflatable do-hickies, more officially known in our house as a "Jumpy Thing." This is a parent's best friend: a fully enclosed, totally padded cube of air, in which your kid can bounce to his or her heart's content, whilst you sit back and relax. It's sort of like an inflatable baby sitter, just not as controversial. (*Helpful Tip: Don't Google "inflatable baby sitter."*)

When we arrived at the Jumpy Thing Place (not the official name), we immediately made a b-line for the lone Jumpy Thing, which was out back next to the bumper boats and the go-carts. My daughter's eyes bulged at the sight of the air-filled cube of ecstasy. But then, just as I was ready to toss her inside and make for the nearest bench, I noticed the interior of the Jumpy Thing was soaking wet and dotted with puddles from the rain earlier that day. Our mutual dreams of Jumpy-Thing bliss were instantly deflated.

Luckily we had one other option: The Indoor Foam-Ball-Filled Giant-Rat-Maze-Like Thing-A-Ma-Jigger (official name). Picture a completely padded, four-story obstacle course for kids, complete with about a million foam balls, and tons of things to climb on, over, and through. The most impressive feature of this particular Thing-A-Ma-Jigger was the twisting tunnel slide, which, when you slid down it, created enough static electricity to power a small city.

For the next hour or so, my six-months-pregnant wife and I followed Boogieface through this monstrous maze of fun, as she explored every nook and cranny. At first, we were simply trying to help her along and make sure she was safe. But it wasn't long before we too were climbing and jumping and sliding with the best of them. At one point, Cassie nearly got stuck between two large foam rollers, which most certainly gave our unborn child a start. If her water had broken, I doubt anyone would have noticed. This plastic-covered contraption had certainly seen its share of sweat, urine, vomit, and other bodily fluids. The proof was in the smell.

By the time we were ready to head home, my daughter was completely happy and – better yet – completely exhausted. She was out before we finished buckling her into her car seat.

So it looks like we may have found another option for indoor family fun this winter. You really can't beat a place where you and your kid can both act like children, and the occasional tumble won't result in any permanent damage to your child's face.

Which is always a plus.

It's Potty Time!

In just two short months my wife and I will be welcoming our second child into the world. Soon we will be a family of four. What this means, according to my friends who already have multiple children, is that our life as we know it will soon be over. Hooray!

In anticipation of this momentous event, my wife and I are doing everything we can to prepare (Ha!) so that we'll be ready (Ha!) when the big moment comes. One thing we've been focusing on is potty training our two-year-old. The way we see it, if we're only changing one child's diapers, it will help us make a smooth transition into this next phase of parenthood (Ha!).

My wife has always claimed that she was diaper-free by 18 months—a statement I verified with my mother-in-law. So, right around 17 months, we began trying to convince our daughter that, despite the inherent convenience of diapers, it's really more fun to go to the bathroom *outside of* your clothing. It seemed like an easy sell, but the little bugger wasn't buying it. Now, here we are at 26 months and counting, and she's still putting up one heck of a fight.

The first thing we did is go out and buy Boogieface her very own Elmo potty, which actually congratulates you, both in English and in Spanish, when you do your thing, so to speak. We had high hopes for this, since Elmo is the Oprah of the toddler world. Unfortunately, not even the idea of having her very own bilingual bedpan was enough to convince her.

Next we tried bribery. We promised her two M&Ms if she went No. 1 and three if she went No. 2. (Personally, I thought that we should do one for No. 1 and two for No. 2, to avoid any confusion, but that's beside the point.) This offer certainly sweetened the deal (sorry), and she actually began to use her potty sporadically. But gradually, even the promise of a chocolaty reward lost its appeal.

Now I've resorted to self-humiliation in order to get her potty-trained. In the rare occasion that she uses her toilet, I demonstrate my approval by jumping up and down like an idiot, which she thoroughly enjoys. Unfortunately, I'm not always at home when she goes. Just recently I received some strange looks at the grocery store when I responded to a text from my wife with a video reply of me jumping around in the canned foods aisle saying, "You went poo-poo on the potty!?!?! YAAAAAAAAY!!!" (The video was for my daughter, lest their be any confusion.)

For now I guess we'll just have to be patient and hope that she takes to the potty training before Baby #2 arrives. If the M&Ms and the jumping up and down fail to do the trick, we may have to resort to cash.

Your generous donations are appreciated.

Fatherhood 2.0

It's coming, and there's no way to stop it. Like a killer asteroid on course to collide with the Earth. And when it finally arrives, life as we know it will cease to exist.

This month my wife and I will be welcoming our second child into the world. And when Baby #2 finally arrives, he or she will be greeted by the big brown eyes of our adorable, two-year-old daughter, who, after initially feigning excitement and happiness, will no doubt begin to devise a devious plan to get back at her little brother or sister for stealing the spotlight. After all, that's what big sisters are for.

Ever since Cassie learned she was pregnant, other parents of two or more children have been congratulating us by informing us just how hellish our lives will be once the little bundle of joy is born. You think your life is crazy now, they say—JUST WAIT! How wonderful to have friends like these to take our joyous anticipation and smash it into oblivion! We're so blessed.

For the past eight-plus months or so, I've been looking forward to the arrival of Baby #2 much like I look forward to my first prostate exam, which, unfortunately, is also looming on the horizon. After all, it's difficult to be excited when, according to every other two-child parent I know, as soon as this new baby is born we'll be so overcome and so exhausted and so busy that we will no longer have time for such luxuries as showering, eating, and breathing.

Then again, maybe I'm just panicking. Is it possible that maybe, just maybe, the parents we've spoken to are exaggerating. I'm no rookie to this fatherhood thing, you know. I've been around the block, and I know what to expect: the sleepless nights, the refusals to eat, the temper tantrums, the poopie diapers, the using of phrases like "poopie diapers", etc. I mean, how much trouble can one little baby cause?

This is what I keep telling myself as we inch closer and closer to The Big Day. But to be honest, it's not working. I'm in full panic mode now. If my brain had one of those Homeland Security color-coded thingies, I'd be right around Code Orange. I'm starting to recall those first weeks after our daughter was born, when I slogged through each day like a zombie, doing stupid things like putting the milk in the cupboard and the cat in the microwave. Just kidding! We don't even have a cat.

It was the dog.

So, good reader, if this is my final transmission, and, according to every other parent I know, there's a good chance it is, please tell the world my story. Tell them I was a good man, husband, and father, and that I tried to do everything I could for my beautiful children, whom I loved dearly, and who, ironically, drove me to an early grave.

Boy, Oh Boy!

"I have to warn you," says the nurse, as she checks my newborn son, just minutes after his arrival. "Watch out when you're changing your little guy's diaper. With boys, as soon as their thingy hits the air, they have a tendency to pee all over." I took out my pen and notepad: Watch out for his "thingy."

And so began life with my son.

Having a son is a lot of pressure on a dad. A daughter is a piece of cake. Mommy dresses her and does her hair, and I just watch from the sidelines, clueless. Oh, once in a while I have to dress up for a tea party or play with dolls, but I really don't have to worry about much until she's a teenager and boys start coming around the house. I've already purchased a large baseball bat for that occasion.

But now that I have a son, I have much more responsibility. It's up to me to teach him all the manly things, like how to use a chainsaw, how to spit properly, and the best way to hold a remote control. This is a lot of pressure for a guy who's never been known as Mr. Masculine. I was raised with two sisters, you see. Growing up, I was surrounded by baby dolls and curling irons and ballet shoes. Honestly, I don't know how I made it out alive.

Luckily, my father did a decent job of making sure I had enough man-type activities in my life. We piled wood together, did yard work together, moved large rocks around together—you know, *guy* stuff. He even taught me how to play sports and, more important, since he *never* let me win, how to be a good loser. My dad did a good job of keeping me in touch with my maleness, even while I was being dragged to my sisters' dance recitals and cheerleader competitions. Those were dark days, indeed.

One thing that concerns me, though, is my son's size. He was 9 lbs., 7 oz., and 22.5 inches long at birth. A voracious eater, he's now well over 11 lbs. And there's no end in sight. I'm barely 6 feet tall, and I've never weighed more than 170 lbs. According to my calculations, at his current growth rate, my boy will be 7 feet tall and 285 lbs. by his 12th birthday, which will make putting him in timeout a real challenge.

So far, I think I'm doing pretty well raising him. I already showed him the proper way to pour a beer, so as not to get too much foam, and I even think he understands the inherent flaws of the prevent defense. Next up, the joy of quoting movies.

And thanks to those words of wisdom from our friendly nurse, my son has only peed on me once so far. Which is nice.

Diaper Daze

"How 'bout I watch Elmo and then I go pee-pee on potty? Good idea?"

When your 2-and-a-half-year-old starts bargaining with you, you know you're in trouble. And that's exactly where we are in the Battle of Potty Training.

Things started off great when we first introduced Boogieface to the joys of indoor plumbing. First we'd plop her down on her kiddie potty and wait a few minutes until she went. Then we'd jump and clap and scream and make a huge deal about it and give her two M&Ms as a reward. It worked brilliantly.

For a while.

Then one day she had an epiphany and realized that using the potty was some lame idea that Mommy and Daddy had come up. Therefore, she wasn't going to do it anymore. This was a great disappointment to us, since we had hoped to complete her potty training before our next child arrived. Buying diapers for one kid is expensive enough; buying for two, we calculated, would cut into our weekly sushi budget, which simply is not an option.

But by the time my son was born, my daughter remained steadfast in her potty boycott.

Now I'm sure there are a lot of you out there – those of you who don't have children – who are saying, "Are you kidding me? She's a toddler. Just pick her up and put her on the toilet, for pete's sake."

Oh. Yeah. Why didn't I think of that? And now back to reality…

Imagine, if you will, trying to get an agitated, rambunctious, 25-pound greased pig to sit still for 10 minutes. Now imagine that same pig is letting loose a blood-curdling, ear-piercing scream. That's what we go through several times each day.

It's a real hoot, let me tell you.

Once, in another moment of desperation, I considered using duct tape to attach her to the toilet. Luckily, I came to my senses and realized just how crazy that would be. Duct tape is way too expensive.

So I guess for now we'll just have to be patient and continue to work at it. If that means I have to bargain with her, so be it. Besides, I'm sure she'll come around sooner or later. I mean, she can't wear diapers forever.

Can she?

That's Not Chocolate!

It was Good Friday and I had the day off, so we decided to take the kids to Eggstravaganza, an annual Easter-themed event at a local church.

Since we were running a little early, we stopped off at Bed, Bath & Beyond to continue the seemingly never-ending search for the perfect curtains.

I could hardly contain my excitement.

As my wife began to peruse the curtains section, I kept a careful eye on the bouncy ball that is my two-and-a-half-year-old, making sure she didn't subject us to the dreaded You-Break-It-You-Bought-It rule.

Suddenly, Boogieface disappeared, lost within the labyrinth that is the curtains section. When I finally located her, it was by smell rather than sight.

"I need you change my diaper change," she said, in her unique, grammar-challenged style, her head poking out from within a rack of curtains. By the look on her face and her wide-legged stance, I could tell it wasn't going to be pretty. Of course, the diaper bag was out in the car, so I ran out to get it as Cassie picked up my son in his carrier and whisked my daughter off to the ladies room.

When I returned with the bag, my wife opened the bathroom door and handed me a very heavy and very smelly diaper. "Dispose of this, please" she said, fighting off a gag. Initially, I considered tossing the baby bio-hazard into the nearest trash can, just to get it out of my hands. But I couldn't bear to do that to the other innocent shoppers in the store. So instead, I quickly made my way outside and deposited the diaper in the street-side can.

Free of the smelly burden, I went back into the store and took a drink from the water fountain as I waited for them to emerge from the restroom.

That's when I felt the wetness.

Looking down at my shorts, I expected to see a spot from some water fountain spillage. Instead, what I saw looked more like melted chocolate.

That's strange, I thought. I wasn't eating any choc… OH NO! I pounded on the door of the ladies room and begged my wife to give me a wipey—STAT!

While I cleaned myself the best I could, I deduced that the diaper must have been leaking when I took it outside to throw it away. I also deduced that if the diaper had leaked on me, it was very likely that it had also dripped on the floor. One look to the ground confirmed my fears, as I saw several wet, brownish dots forming a distinct dotted line to the store's exit.

Just then, Cass and the kids came out of the ladies room, and Boogieface proudly announced to all within earshot, "I pooped on Daddy!" As a muffled laughter spread across the store, I discreetly told my wife about the chocolate-colored trail on the ground.

"Take care of it—NOW!" she demanded.

So, as the three of them exited the store, I went from dot to dot, quickly wiping away the evidence. Shortly thereafter, we were at Target buying Daddy a new pair of shorts. It was an inauspicious beginning to what turned out to be a wonderful day.

I'm just glad I didn't try to taste the chocolate.

Infantile Humor

My son is a comedian. Granted, he's only six months old, but believe me, he's a real jokester.

For example, for the first four months after he was born, he slept through the night without a peep. We'd put him down for the night around 9 p.m. and he'd sleep solid until 6 o'clock the next morning. It was blissful.

Then, just to be funny, he started waking up three times a night to eat. Ha! What a kidder!

When you have a baby that doesn't sleep right from the start, at least you know what to expect. But when you have one that gets you used to a full night's sleep and then suddenly rips the rug out from under your feet, that's just plain cruel. In times like these, you become desperate and will consider anything in order to get a full night of shuteye, like red wine mixed in with the baby's milk.

I'm just kidding, of course! You can't mix wine and milk!

I just give him the wine straight up.

Another one of my son's favorite jokes is waiting for me to take off his diaper and then shooting a warm stream of urine right into my eye. That one really cracks me up, let me tell you! You hear people with baby boys say that they've been peed on, you imagine a gently flowing stream trickling out of the diaper like a peaceful, babbling brook. This is not the case. Imagine instead an out of control fire hose or maybe Old Faithful. It's as if his thingy is air-activated or something.

Someone gave us a tiny knitted cap for the little guy's "little guy" that you're supposed to use when changing his diaper in order to protect you from getting sprayed. But it just shoots off like a urine-propelled rocket ship.

When I finally regain control of the situation, urine is dripping from all surfaces within a five-foot radius. Meanwhile, my son just lies there in a pool of his own pee, smiling and giggling at dear old Dad's expense. He could do stand-up, that one, if only he could stand up.

Yeah, he's a funny little dude. Let's see how funny he thinks it is when we trade him in for a housebroken labradoodle that sleeps through the night.

Snips and Snails and Puppy Dog Tails

When it came to diapering my daughter, I was a pro. I could de-diaper her, clean whatever needed to be cleaned, and re-diaper her in a matter of seconds. It became a thing of pride. I'd challenge myself to be quicker and more efficient with every change. Sometimes I'd imagine I was a one-man tire-changing machine and she was a race car (a really cute one) that just pulled into the pits. Only the "tires" were actually Pampers.

Then along came my son.

I heard it from day one: Boys are sooooooo different than girls! This warning was repeated again and again…and again. But besides acknowledging the obvious differences in biological equipment, I had a hard time believing that he would be that much different than my daughter. I mean, they came from the same factory and were made with the same parts (well, almost). How different could they really be?

Take changing diapers, for example. Boogieface would always lie perfectly still during the process. It was like diapering a baby doll. My son, on the other hand, is incapable of stillness. He writhes around and squirms the entire time, and with surprising strength, too. You ever see a rodeo, when the cowboys try to wrastle a steer to the ground and subdue it by tying its hooves together? It's sort of like that, only the steer is a baby boy and you don't have any rope.

The main problem is, being a human being, I only have two hands. With my left hand, I hold his ankles together and try to keep him still. Then, with my right hand, I undo his diaper, get a wipey to clean him, and then lay him on top of the new diaper. Meanwhile, my son arches his back and twists his body to one side in an attempt to escape and locate the nearest electrical cord to chew on. This can be especially troublesome if, say, he leaves me a "present" in his diaper. Let's just leave it at that.

Now, if I were an orangutan, changing his diaper would be a piece of cake. I could hold him down with my hands and change his diaper using my dexterous feet. Then again, if I were an orangutan, I doubt any woman would have agreed to have children with me in the first place.

My wife's perfected a method where she actually uses her feet to hold him down by his shoulders while she quickly changes his diaper. It's quite ingenious, really. I tried this method once, but it was just too awkward for someone as inflexible as me. I can barely touch my toes, for pete's sake.

And it's not just the diapering that's different. My son also gets into and climbs on things way more than my daughter ever did. Also, when he plays with something, first he examines the toy or object by putting it into his mouth, which my daughter did as well, but then he shakes it around violently, like an angry Rottweiler with a helpless bunny rabbit, before finally throwing it across the room. And when it comes to eating, the boy is a voracious, toothless, bottomless pit of hunger. He's like a goat. All I can say is, when he starts eating, keep your hands to your sides, lest you lose a finger.

He's like an animal, really. In fact, I think that's what I'll call him from now on: The Animal. As they say, call a spade a spade.

(Spading…hmmm? I wonder if that would…nah.)

Excuse Me, Ma'am, But There's a Binky in My Bisque

I used to be one of those people. You know, the kind who give the evil eye to parents who dare bring their young kids to a restaurant. After all, how can you enjoy a good meal with someone else's annoying kids screaming their heads off the whole time? My kids would never act that way, I used to say.

Well, the years went by and soon I was blessed with my own little munchkins to look after. Now the shoe's on the other foot, so to speak. Now my wife and I are the inconsiderate parents who bring their children to the restaurant and disturb everyone around us. At least, that's what we think you're thinking. Who am I kidding? I know that's what you're thinking.

And you know what? We don't care.

Look, you try staying at home and eating in every single night with an infant and a toddler. Believe me—it gets old really quick. Going out to a restaurant is one of our only escapes. It's a last desperate attempt to pretend that we still have a life and that we're still members of the community. And if it means that we have to endure your dirty looks and not-so-private snide remarks, well…so be it. We want our sushi!

I'm sorry. Forgive me. I don't know what got into me. I've just been a little stressed out lately. You know…kids.

It's not that I don't understand your frustration. Like I said, I've been there. When we're at a local eatery, and The Animal is screaming and pounding his hands on the table, over and over again, smashing his peas into oblivion, I feel your pain. When Boogieface is jumping up and down in the booth, and she's peering over the partition to stare at you and make you feel completely uncomfortable, I understand your frustration. Really, I do. I may not appear concerned, as I relish each bite of my crab cakes and treasure each sip of Cabernet, trying to pretend that these aren't my children—but believe me, I feel your pain.

Does this mean that I'm going to stop going out to eat at nice restaurants? Ha! Of course not. Like I said, Daddy needs his sushi. Deal with it.

OK, again, I'm sorry. I'm usually not so rude. It's just that my wife and I have always loved going out to eat, and we just can't fathom giving it up until our kids are older and less prone to erratic, outrageous behavior. Believe me, if Chuck E. Cheese had eggplant parmesan or New York strip, we'd just as soon go there and let the little ones scream their heads off.

But as long as the restaurant has a "Kids' Menu," I'm eating there. Don't like it? Stay at home!

Again, I apologize. I guess I'm just worn out. And hungry.

Anyone know a good place to eat?

The Return of Christmas

When I was younger, like most kids, I was rabid about Christmas. The calendar year would fly by at its normal pace until December 1, and then it would decelerate to a crawl as I waited for that glorious day to arrive. Every Sunday at Mass during Advent, I'd count the remaining candles, wishing that I could just go into a coma and awake on Christmas morning, refreshed and ready to tear into my presents.

Finally, Christmas Eve would arrive—the longest day of the year, by far (forget June 21)—and my family and I would head to church. The Christmas Eve service would move at a glacial pace, as hundreds of casual church-goers joined us regulars and packed the pews like sardines. We'd have to get there an hour early just go get a seat, which made it all the more torturous. With so many people packed inside, oxygen was at a premium, and during the service people would be dropping like flies. You didn't always see them fall, but you could tell when another one went down by the unmistakable sound of head striking pew.

At the end of Mass—if you survived that long—the organist would strike up a rousing rendition of "Joy to the World." It was the only song all year that everyone in the church actually sang enthusiastically. Then we'd head off to begin our respective Christmas Eve traditions.

Ours took place at my grandparents' house, where Grandma's ham had been cooking for hours, filling the entire house with that delicious honey-glazed aroma. I couldn't care less about the ham, however; I was itching to get at the mountain of presents that awaited my sisters and me in the living room. Of course, my parents and grandparents would drag out dinner as long as they could until our incessant whining would cause them to cave in. Then we'd stampede into the other room to discover what treasures awaited us.

The next morning, my little sister and I would awake before dawn and head into the living room where our presents sat, gently illuminated by the soft, multi-colored glow of the Christmas tree. Immediately we'd start counting the number of presents in our piles and try to guess their contents. We always felt bad for our older sister, whose stack of gifts always contained the most flat, rectangular boxes, i.e., clothes. Of course the best presents were in the odd-shaped boxes that held some kind of toy waiting to be released from its clear-plastic prison.

Finally—and I do mean FINALLY—my parents and older sister would drag themselves out of bed and join us in the living room to let the Christmas festivities begin. In a flash the unwrapping frenzy would be over, and I'd be admiring the newest additions to my toy collection: Star Wars figures, G.I. Joes, Transformers, Matchbox and Hot Wheels die-cast cars, and all the other wonders that captured the fancy of young boys during the 1980s. Then it was off to my other Grandma's to collect even more Christmas booty. (Yes, I was spoiled.)

Somewhere along the line, however, Christmas lost its magic. Grandma and Pappap passed away, traditions changed, and G.I. Joes and Matchbox cars no longer filled me with wonder. Eventually I found new traditions and new ways to celebrate the season with family and friends, but that feeling, the one I used to have as a kid, I thought I'd lost it forever.

But now that's all changed. Now I have a three-year-old and an 11-month-old, and suddenly I'm excited about Christmas again. Now, once again, I have that feeling—that giddy anticipation that used to have me dreaming about cap guns and toy trains and remote-control cars. Only now, I'm also dreaming about dolls and play kitchen sets and all the other things that make my daughter's eyes light up. Now I'm driving her to daycare and belting out Christmas favorites like "Frosty" and "Rudolph" and "the one about the list" (as she calls it) over and over…and over again. Now I know that soon they too will be counting down those excruciatingly long December days as they dream about what they'll find when they come down the stairs on Christmas morning and wait, in agony, for Mom and Dad to "get up already!"

The feeling is back. It's a Christmas miracle.

Father-Daughter Bonding...In the Men's Room

So my wife and I take the kids to one of our favorite haunts the other day, Mario's—home of fine Italian cuisine and a loud, bustling atmosphere that enables someone with young children to blend in, unheard and unnoticed.

While Cassie spooned a jar of blended chicken, veggies, and who-knows-what-else into our ever-ravenous son's mouth, Boogieface scribbled miniature Picassos on Daddy's pocket notebook.

"Here, Daddy...for you!" she said, handing me a perfect rendering of a shapeless blob.

I paused and admired the crude but unique work of art. "For me? Thank you, sweetheart!"

"No, Daddy, it goes this way," she said, taking the drawing from my hand and turning it 180 degrees.

"Oh! Of course," I said. "My mistake."

As we waited for our food to arrive, Boogs suddenly popped out of her chair. "I have to go pee-pee."

"Let's go!" I said, grabbing her by the hand and whisking her away to the men's room. You have to act quick in these situations; you never know how much time you may have.

Seconds later, she was finished doing her business—or so I thought. "I have to go POO-pee, too!"

At home my daughter prefers a little privacy when nature calls. She always tells me to "Go out!" and "Shut the door—ALL THE WAY!!" But here, in the noisy restaurant, I didn't think I'd be able to hear her outside, and I didn't want to leave her alone. "Do you want me to turn around and face the wall so you can go?" I asked.

"Yeah," she replied. "And close your eyes."

So, for the next 15 minutes—yes, 15 minutes—I stood there, eyes closed, facing the wall as my little girl sang songs and did her thing on the potty. Of course, she wouldn't have known whether my eyes were really closed or not, but honestly, I didn't want to jinx it. Meanwhile, customers knocked on the door to no avail, wondering what the hold-up was.

Finally, she said she was done, and so I proceeded with the wiping. "Make sure you throw the paper in the basket over there," she said, "not in the potty." I immediately understood why: she wanted to see her creation. I flatly denied her request, of course, mainly out of consideration to future restroom visitors.

Walking back to our table, and to my now cold food, I could see that my wife was wondering what had taken so long. But before I could explain, Boogieface made a gleeful and audible announcement to my wife and the entire restaurant: "I WENT POO-PEE!!!"

Luckily, due to the noise, only a couple dozen people heard her. Otherwise it could have been embarrassing.

I can't wait to share this story with my daughter years from now. Preferably when she's entertaining a male suitor.

Teach Your Children Well

As a parent, it's your duty to impart your wisdom on your children; to share with them the many things you've learned during your time on this planet. This includes basic things like how to brush your teeth, how to tie your shoes, how to blow your nose, and so forth. It also includes teaching them proper manners and how to act in different situations—things that will help them function in society as they go about their own life's journey.

You also want to teach your kids about things that are important to you. Such as how to do the "Crüe" sign.

Being an avid fan of Motley Crüe, the prototypical "hair band" of the 1980s, I felt compelled to share my devotion with my daughter. She was still wearing diapers when I began showing her how to pump her fist in the air and chant "Crüe! Crüe! Crüe!", just as I have done at many a concert over the years. Boogieface quickly mastered this skill, even though it sounded more like "Cwüe! Cwüe! Cwüe!" But I knew that would come in time.

Some people might think it strange or even reprehensible to teach someone so young about a band known for its leather-clad members, controversial lyrics, and disturbing imagery. To them I say: Have you ever seen and episode of "Barney"? Talk about disturbing.

I had all but forgotten about this early lesson in Hair Bands 101, when, just the other day, Boogieface called out to me as I loaded the dishwasher. "Look, Daddy," she said, seated at the dining room table, "Cwüe! Cwüe! Cwüe!" I turned to see her grinning widely as she pumped her tiny little fist in the air—a future head-banger in the making. It brought a tear to my eye.

Then, one day last week after picking her up from day care, I was going through the channels on my satellite radio when I happened upon the Death Metal station. This is the type of music where it sounds like the lead singer is dry heaving to a symphony of wood chippers.

"Leave this on, Daddy!" Boogs chimed in from her car seat in the back.

"This song?" I asked. "You like *this* song?" I saw her nod in the rearview mirror. The big softy that I am, I figured, what the heck? If she likes this type of music, so be it. But as the lead singer vomited out more lyrics, I wondered if it was appropriate for a three-year-old's ears. "How about I see if something else is on?"

"NO, DADDY!" she cried. "Don't turn it—PLEEEAASE!!"

Hey, don't blame me. All I did was show her how to pump her fist in the air.

So, as the soothing sounds of Death Metal echoed inside my Hyundai, I realized that, no matter how much we teach them or try to get them to be like us, our kids will end up having their own unique personality and interests.

Besides, it could have been worse. We could have been listening to Barney.

Ravenous Readers

Anyone who knows me knows I love to read. I go through about 40 books a year on average, and I always make sure to have a book with me so that I can squeeze in a page or two whenever I can. Heck, I even read while I'm walking. Chalk it up as just another one of my many unique and utterly useless skills (along with the ability to hum and whistle at the same time).

We started reading books to my daughter within days of bringing her home from the hospital. It was my wife's idea. Personally, I thought it a bit bizarre, considering my daughter could barely see, and she didn't comprehend English yet. We might as well have been reading to the wall.

Today, more than three and a half years later, Boogieface is a true bibliophile, just like her daddy. In all that time, not a night has gone by that we haven't read her at least one book before bed. Sometimes we read the same book two or three times. As a result, I can now recite *Goodnight Moon* backwards. In my sleep.

When The Animal was born, we planned on doing the same thing with him. Unfortunately, he suffers from a chronic malady commonly known as Second Child Syndrome. Because of this we have about half as many pictures of him than we had of my daughter. We also tend to "forget" about him occasionally, only to find him eating out of the garbage can or grooming himself with the toilet brush.

And although we intended on reading to him every night, as we did with my daughter, we just never got into the habit.

So as soon as he could walk, my son took matters into his own hand and started bringing the books to us. It's really cute. He goes over to his little book shelf, picks out one of his favorites, and then toddles over to us saying "Book! Book!" Then, after we read it to him, he goes and gets another book from the shelf and does it all over again. And again.

And again.

The boy devours books—literally. One time while he was sitting in the corner reading, I stepped out for a moment, and when I came back in, all that was left was a soggy book spine and some shreds of paper.

I think it's wonderful that we're developing two voracious readers. It develops your imagination and opens up your mind to a whole new world of discovery and learning.

Plus, a book is a heck of a lot cheaper than a Nintendo DS.

C is for Cookie (And Crazy, Too)

I have an iPhone that holds my entire music collection. I also have a satellite radio subscription. So when I'm in my car, I literally have hundreds of my favorite songs at my disposal. But lately the only thing I've been rockin' out to is "Rubber Duckie."

On a recent road trip, Cass and I went against our No Kiddie Music in the Car rule in order to keep our two little kiddos happy, i.e., quiet, during the ride. The only thing is, now Boogieface expects it anytime we go anywhere. Sometimes I try to trick her into forgetting about "her music," as she calls it. Tuning in to the all-'80s channel, I start nodding my head to the beat.

"Good song, huh?" I say, as Toto's "Africa" fills the cabin.

"I want MY music," she replies flatly, her pouty yet irresistibly cute face glaring at me through the rearview mirror. And so I give in and hit play as the oh-too-familiar voice of Cookie Monster belts out "C is for Cookie"—a song that will worm itself into my brain for the remainder of the day.

And it's not just music. When you have young kids, you can kiss any type of relaxation goodbye. The moment you think you have a few moments of solitude, a voice calls out to you through the baby monitor; a cry rings out on the other side of the bathroom door, begging to come in; a plea comes from the back seat of the car, asking you to turn off the sports-talk radio for a bunch of singing puppets.

I used to get up a little early so I could gradually emerge from my slumber, while taking in the morning news and watching SportsCenter.

Now, I still wake up early, but it's because The Animal is calling for me and shaking his crib violently, like some sort of caged wild animal.

When I take him downstairs, I try to buy me a little more "me" time. "Here, buddy. Come play with your toys," I say, plopping him in front of his toy box, as I plop myself on the sofa and grab the remote. But of course he has other plans for me. Ignoring his toys, he goes straight for his books, which, for the next half hour or so, he brings over to me one by one.

"BOOK! BOOK!" he says, holding out *Go, Dog! Go!*, his favorite literary work. Then he clambers up on my lap and waits with giddy anticipation. All I really want to do is zone out with the tube, but I just can't say no to my little book-loving (sometimes book-eating) buddy. I'm a writer, after all; he may be a future reader of mine.

So nowadays my only "me" time comes long after the kiddos are sound asleep. After I've finished cleaning the kitchen and folding the laundry and paying the bills and doing all the other tedious grown-up duties I didn't have time for earlier in the day, I'm left with about 15 minutes or so of down time until I trudge up to bed, "C is for Cookie" on repeat in my brain.

But it's all good. I may not have much time for myself anymore, but I know that one day soon, I'll look back on these years with longing, wishing that my daughter still wanted to listen to Sesame Street's greatest hits and that my son wanted me to read *Moo, Baa, La La La!* to him. Again.

For the thousandth time.

My Life as a Border Collie

During the journey of fatherhood, you go through different phases. Phase #1 is the Maybe-We-Made-A-BIG-Mistake phase. Then there's Phase #2, the This-Isn't-So-Bad-After-All phase. Then, after your second child is born, you enter Phase #3, the I-Can't-Believe-We-Let-This-Happen-AGAIN! phase.

Right now I'm in Phase #4, the Border Collie Phase. My main responsibility these days is chasing after my 18-month-old and herding him away from potential dangers and things that he could break, which basically includes everything in his general vicinity.

Much like a Border Collie runs alongside the sheep, herding them away from the cliff's edge and into the safety of the pen, I must continually shadow The Animal, running alongside him to make sure he doesn't eat the dog food, drink out of another kid's sippy cup, or carve out a swath of destruction. It's exhausting work.

For his age, my son is surprisingly quick, deceptively so. And he's crafty, too. He'll get your attention by reaching for the bowl of Alpo in the corner. Then, as you dart over to grab the bowl and put it out of reach, he's already off and running towards his real target—your piping hot cup of coffee, which you foolishly left within toddler-eye-view over on the end table. So you dash back across the room and dive for the coffee, clumsily knocking it over and spilling it onto the carpet below. By this time The Animal is already on his way to the bathroom with the remote control, which he will then toss into the toilet.

Along with your toothbrush.

When you're dealing with a wild creature like this, you can forget about going anywhere. Inside our home we control him by barricading him within a Danger-Free Zone in the living room. But once we step out outside the zone, all bets are off.

Recently I took him to a graduation party for one of my cousins. Shouldn't be too hard, I thought. I'll just get a plate of food, walk around, and let my son explore the yard, taking advantage of the many doting relatives who will undoubtedly keep him occupied whilst I gorge myself on fried chicken, baked beans, and haluski.

But just as I began to survey the buffet table, The Animal took off for the three decorative glass thingamabobs in the flower garden. "NO!" I snapped, quickly removing his hand from one of the fragile works of art. Of course he immediately went for the next one in line, and then the next one. "I SAID NO TOUCH!!" I yelled, as he darted around the back of the house, searching for some backyard pond to bathe in or some extension cord to chew on. Like a good Border Collie, I followed in hot pursuit.

Meanwhile, my relatives were enjoying the show as they relaxed and savored the delicious graduation party fare. I kept waiting for some adoring great aunt or compassionate cousin to swoop in like a hawk, take The Animal off my hands, and give me a few precious moments to attack the tray of boneless chicken wings that were calling my name from the buffet. But alas, no one came to my rescue. We were only there for about 45 minutes when I grabbed my boy and headed for home, exhausted, sweaty, and starving.

Who knows how long this phase will last? All I know is I'm running out of energy, and I need to think of a way to keep my son under control.

Anyone have a dog cage I can borrow?

Daddy's Little Demon

"Just hold the dress open and I'll shove her down into it!" I said to my wife.

We were late in leaving for a wedding, one in which Boogieface was to be the flower girl. However, at the moment she was a demonic creature from the Netherworld. And she was dead set against putting on that dress.

Just moments before I had been up street picking out a wedding card when my phone rang. It was Cassie, and she sounded desperate.

"Get home as soon as you can," she said. "We have a situation here." So I paid for the card and sped home, not sure what to expect when I got there.

Cass greeted me at the door. "I'm going to kill her," she said. "Really. I'm not kidding this time." I looked over and saw my screaming, sobbing, hysterical little girl, sitting in the corner of the dining room, wearing nothing but her tights.

Obviously I needed to diffuse the situation. "Go get ready," I said. "I'll handle it." My wife's "tough cop" routine may have failed, but surely my fatherly charms could soothe my frantic first-born.

So, crouching down to her level and speaking in a clear, composed voice, I told her that she had to put the dress on because she had a very special part in the wedding, and that the dress would make her look like a princess!

But the demon was unmoved. "I am NOT putting on my dress!!"

Again, I reiterated her obligation to the bride and groom and clearly explained the urgency of our situation. "Listen, Boogs, I don't know what's wrong, but we're going to be late. So, I'm very sorry, but you're going to have to put on your dress. OK?"

That's when the screaming hit a new, ear-splitting level. "I! WILL! NOT! PUT! IT! OOOOOOOOOOON!!!!!!!!!!!!"

There comes a moment in parenting when, no matter how hard you try to remain calm, your blood begins to boil. You can feel it, slowly rising up from your belly and radiating into your chest. One minute you're in total control of your emotions; the next, you're the Incredible Hulk, and you feel as if you could pick up the television and throw it through the window—and it would feel really, really good!

We had reached this critical moment.

"YOU *WILL* PUT IT ON!" I said, fire and smoke emanating from my mouth. "RIGHT NOW!"

"NO...I...WON'T!!!"

Since diplomacy had obviously failed, I decided it was time for Plan B—Operation Stuff Her in the Dress. And it wasn't easy, what with her screaming and hitting and kicking the entire time. Then, just as we managed to cram her into the dress, she activated the one super-power that all kids have, where they can instantly triple their body weight and drop to the floor like an anvil.

But we were not deterred. While taking blow after blow to the face, Cass, the trooper she is, managed to squeeze Boogieface's feet into her white patent-leather shoes. Then I immediately whisked the screeching demon...I mean, my daughter, outside and strapped her into her car seat. All the while the neighbors peered out from behind their venetian blinds, horrified.

As Cassie and I attended to our wounds, we expected a long drive ahead of us, one full of screaming and crying. But amazingly, just minutes down the road, Boogieface was somehow exorcised of the demon and transformed back into our little angel. It was a miracle! Either that or she could sense wedding cookies in her future and, therefore, abruptly changed her tune.

Somehow we made it to the church on time and my beautiful princess walked down the aisle as the wedding guests looked on adoringly. And none of them had any clue that this sweet little cherub had earlier been a crazed demon.

But we have the scars to prove it.

Into the Mystic

You always remember the "firsts" in your life. Your first kiss. Your first car. Your first colonoscopy (not really looking forward to that one). Well, last week we celebrated Boogieface's fourth birthday, and for her big gift she got her first brand-new bicycle.

Previously she'd been riding around on a beat-up old two-wheeler that someone had put out in the trash. Sure, technically it was garbage. But like the old saying goes, one man's trash is another man's chance to save a few bucks.

When my daughter's birthday rolled around, my in-laws wanted to get her something special (i.e., not garbage), so they took her down to the local bike shop and let her pick one out.

I'll never forget my first new bike. It was a Raleigh Rampar—a humble yet rugged two-wheeler with a midnight-blue frame, knobby black tires, and shiny gold handlebars. It was a solid machine that carried me many a mile along the tarred-gravel surface of my neighborhood street. It finally saw its undoing one day when I failed to clear the fabled dirt jump on the old Center Lane trails. Upon impact, the handlebars were stripped and the frame was bent beyond repair. It was a sad yet fitting end to a loyal and dear friend.

For her first bike, Boogieface chose a purple Trek Mystic, complete with oversized tires, training wheels, and a handy handlebar basket. I have to admit, when I found out it was a Trek, I was a little jealous. I mean, don't kids ride Huffys anymore? Then again, I didn't have to pay for it. So good for her!

My little girl sure is adorable, pedaling around the driveway and smiling from ear to ear; her cute little head swaying to and fro beneath the weight of her ridiculously large bike helmet. She's not crazy about the helmet, and I can't say I blame her. Back in my day (oh boy...here we go) we didn't have to wear helmets, which we thought were unnecessary and, quite honestly, dorky. Of course, we also thought stone-washed jeans were cool. So what did we know?

I find it bitter sweet watching my little angel ride around on her new bike. Seems like she's growing up so fast. Next thing you know the training wheels will be off and she'll be cruising down the street with her friends. Before long I'll be watching her pull down the driveway in her first car. Then she'll be heading off to college, where she'll fall in love with some greasy boy who rides a motorcycle. And then I'll be fighting back the tears as I walk her down the aisle and give her away to Mr. Motorcycle, who's completely oblivious to the fact that he's taking my little girl away from me; the one whose diapers I changed and who I used to read to every night before bed, and who I taught to ride a bike in the driveway oh so many years ago.

I know my daughter is only four, but I can't help it—this is how my brain works. I swear these birthdays are going to be the death of me.

The Battle of Dinnertime

"More thoy thauce, peas!" says my son, the salty brown liquid running down his chin and dripping onto his filthy plastic bib. Just moments before, he put the tiny dish of soy sauce up to his mouth and slurped it down like leftover milk in a bowl of cereal. We had given it to him to use as dip for his stew, which he was refusing to eat. A bizarre combination of food and condiment, for sure, but it worked. And, really, that's all that matters.

I used to look forward to dinnertime. It was a time to relax after a long day at work; a time to converse with my wife over a delicious meal as we recalled the day's events. We'd eat slowly, savoring every bite as we cleared our weary minds. Afterward, we'd enjoy a hot cup of coffee and maybe even some dessert. Yep, those were the days!

And now they're long gone.

Now from the moment I secure The Animal in his high chair and connect the Velcro ends of his bib strap, I can feel the anxiety rising within my chest. That's because I know what's coming, and it's not going to be pretty.

Here's a typical dinnertime scenario:

After I set the table and get the kids in their seats, Cass brings out the meal, which she has so kindly prepared for us after putting in a long day of work herself. My ever-ravenous son squeals with excitement, while my daughter looks on, warily. Then my wife places the meal on the table, at which point The Animal's squeals intensify. Across the table Boogieface inevitably falls back into her chair with disappointment since the meal isn't chocolate cake or ice cream. I blow on my son's portion to cool it off, which makes me light-headed and nauseous.

Then, as soon as I place his food on his tray, his squealing stops as his appetite suddenly disappears. "No like it!" he says, shoving the bowl precariously close to the edge. Realizing that the fuse has been lit, Cass and I quickly say grace and begin to fill our plates. I inhale my meal in a matter of seconds, fully expecting my son's sippy cup to come flying at my temple at any moment. Between bites, Cass bickers with our daughter over exactly how much she has to eat before she can be excused. Ten minutes later I'm already in the kitchen cleaning up, i.e., escaping, as my wailing son throws his milk and thrashes around in his high chair. Meanwhile my wife is still trapped in a heated and seemingly endless debate with a four-year-old.

So when we discovered by accident one day that giving The Animal soy sauce would entice him to eat, and, in turn, enable us to do the same, we didn't ask questions. Soy sauce on pizza? Sure! Mixed in with spaghetti? Why not!

As for Boogs, at first she refuses to eat at all. Then, when she realizes her protest is cutting into her valuable play time, she begins to bargain with us. "I know," she says, "how about I eat three more bites, then I can be done?" We counter her offer by saying she has to eat five. "Three!" she replies, sticking to her guns. This goes on and on until finally we give in, exhausted and browbeaten by a preschooler.

The Number of Bites method is just one way that my daughter tries to get out of eating. Sometimes she's struck with a sudden stomachache, which inexplicably disappears once we mention we have ice cream for dessert. Other times she claims she's "just not hungry," even though she hasn't eaten in over three days. Most of the time, though, she just whines and cries until Cass and I, weary and desperate for a peaceful meal, wave the white flag in defeat.

Of course, when it's time to put her to bed, Boogieface's appetite miraculously reappears and she begs us for a bowl of cereal—anything to postpone going to sleep.

It's not fair. When you're a kid, you can eat and sleep as much as you want, but you don't want to. Then, when you're an adult, all you want to do is eat and sleep but you can't.

Somewhere up there God's have a good laugh at our expense.

Scarlett Fever

Parenthood is certainly not for the faint of heart or, when it comes to diapers, the delicate of nose. This is especially true during the first few years, when the exhausting days, sleepless nights, airborne mashed potatoes, temper tantrums, and unpredictable bodily functions – theirs, not yours – can make you wonder if you'll ever get your normal life back again.

You won't.

But if you're able to survive these trying first years, things do get better. Honestly.

Right now, for example, I'm entering into what I call the Brainwashing Phase. My kids have reached the point where I'm comfortable exposing them to things a little more sophisticated than *Moo, Baa, La La La!*, Sesame Street, and [insert any Pixar movie]. Now I can begin teaching them about the finer things in life, i.e., all the things that Daddy likes.

For example, recently my kids got me up early on a Saturday morning and, since I was still burning off some cheap Cabernet from the previous evening, I decided it would be beneficial for us all to veg-out in front of the tube for a while. This usually means me sitting there with a cup of coffee while the kids watch some lame modern cartoon, which inevitably has some sort of boring lesson to teach. When I was a kid (here we go again) the only things cartoons taught us were that 1) coyotes were anvil-proof and basically indestructible; and 2) "wascally wabbits" could always outsmart grumpy, mustachioed, gunslinging prospectors and bald, speech-impaired hunters. But I digress…

On this particular morning, however, as I browsed the TV listings, I noticed that "Gone with the Wind" had just started. A sucker for classic flicks and anything involving the Civil War, I ignored my kids' pleas for "Dora the Explorer" and instead made a date with Vivien Leigh. To my surprise, the kids' whining halted and they immediately became transfixed. To a parent, silence truly is golden, so I tried not to make any sudden movements that might awaken my offspring from their peaceful trance.

After a few minutes, though, I started to feel guilty and clicked the remote to something a little more kid-appropriate. But my kids vehemently protested. "No, Daddy!" they cried out in unison. "Put it back on!" Boogieface told me she liked the dresses that all the Southern belles were wearing. I have no idea what The Animal liked about the movie, considering he can barely speak. But I assume he was intrigued by the film's commentary on the horrors of war and the true meaning of love.

For the next couple of hours, the three of us sat there together on the sofa, coffee and sippy cups in hand, as that romantic and tragic tale of the Old South played out before us. It was wonderful. There were no squeaky cartoon voices, no onslaught of primary colors, no clichéd lessons about sharing. Just Rhett and Scarlett and Melanie and Mammy, all caught up in a whirlwind of love, longing, and the Lost Cause.

When Cassie came downstairs, she was concerned that such mature subject matter might be inappropriate. But I insisted that I was old enough to watch it, so she let it be.

From here on out, the sky's the limit. Now that I've discovered that my kids and I share similar interests, I've decided it's time to introduce them to Daddy's other passions, like coffee, Star Wars, and cryptozoology. Although, it may take some time to explain to them the difference between a Wookie and a Sasquatch. But then, that's what dad's are for, right?

You may disapprove of my parenting style. But frankly, my dear, I don't give a [BLEEP].

It's My Wonderful Life

It sounded like a good idea. Take a 23-month-old to a two-hour-long, black-and-white, largely dialogue-driven movie, right smack in the middle of dinner time.

On second thought, no it didn't.

As part of our ongoing efforts to establish some Christmas traditions, Cassie and I took Boogieface and The Animal to The Strand Theater for a matinee showing of one of my favorite movies, "It's a Wonderful Life." We knew Boogs would like the movie, because it features one of her favorite songs: "Buffalo Gals." And since television usually puts The Animal into a calm, sedated, zombie-like state, we figured the large movie screen would only amplify the effect and put our little guy into a nice, quiet coma. Or so we hoped.

We strategically selected seats up in the balcony in order to distance ourselves from the crowd. But the theater soon filled up, and we found ourselves hemmed in on every side, our escape routes blocked.

As the opening credits rolled on the screen, my kids' eyes locked onto the bright rectangle before them, and I crossed my fingers.

For a while things were fine. Boogs sat quietly at my side, sipping her Sierra Mist; The Animal also seemed content, resting in the warmth of his mother's embrace. But then, just as George and Mary Charlestoned their way into the high school swimming pool, my son's hound-dog-like olfactory system detected the scent of food.

"Want popcorn!" he said loudly, a hint of desperation in his tone. Cassie and I exchanged glances, and I immediately understood my mission: Get popcorn—STAT! By the time Donna Reed was hiding inside the hydrangeas, I was back with two bags, which I hoped would keep my little guy busy for a while.

But we both knew the time bomb was ticking.

Then, just as the "run" began on the Bailey Building and Loan, ironically, The Animal felt a sudden urge to run, too. Having devoured both bags of popcorn, he was now re-energized and restless. Squirming free of Cassie's grasp, he tried to escape down her end of the aisle but was stopped cold by her leg. Without hesitation, he made a break for my side and met the same obstruction. The Animal was trapped. Or so we thought.

Just as George and Mary shared an emotional embrace in their soggy honeymoon suite, The Animal barked something unintelligible, which echoed throughout the theater. It sounded like the noise the velociraptors make in "Jurassic Park" when they're calling the others to come in for the kill.

I could feel the vexation of my fellow moviegoers as they glared in our direction, so I scooped up my boy and made a b-line for the nearest exit.

After chasing him back and forth from the rear-exit stairway to the water fountains and back several times, I decided I had to find another way to wait out the movie. So out into the blustery December night we went, he in his cozy winter coat; me in my flimsy zip-up sweatshirt. My coat was in my car, which was locked; the keys, of course, were up in the balcony with Cassie. And since there's no way we could go back in – literally, they locked the door behind us – I would have to just tough it out, which is not exactly my forte.

For the next hour or so, The Animal happily hopped down Zelienople's main thoroughfare peering in the windows of the town's stores, which were all closed for the night. Meanwhile I played Border Collie, trying to keep him from darting out into the street. At one point, he climbed up onto a porch, stuck his head through the railing, and said to me, "Want ice cream?" I thought he was pretty darn cute, so I played along. "Sure!" I said. "I'll take some." Two seconds later he returned with my "ice cream": a dirty ash tray.

After the movie, Cass and Boogieface found us across the street in an Italian restaurant, where I was attempting to defrost with a glass of cheap red wine. For the moment, The Animal was calm, his attention held by a Grover picture e-book he was reading on my iPhone, which, by the way, he was smearing with his ketchup-covered, French-fry-greasy fingers.

But despite being cold and tired and frustrated, and besides having to woof down my dinner while defending myself and the other patrons from flying salt shakers and other 23-month-old-powered projectiles, I have to admit, it really is a wonderful life.

Just next time I think we'll rent the DVD.

Pet Rocks and Toy Animal Urinals

"Where my Oink and my Moo?" asks The Animal, searching the house for his two favorite toys, a wooden pig and cow, which are actually just handles from broken ice cream spoons.

"Can I keep it and take it home?" asks my daughter, picking up a large rock next to a sidewalk planter. She has a gazillion baby dolls, but Boogieface desperately wanted to adopt this new "pet", which she then thoroughly washed in the bathroom sink, wrapped in a wipey, and then decorated with a purple barrette.

Our home is a garbage dump of plastic, Made-in-China, primary-color madness. It's an orphanage for literally dozens of baby dolls of every shape and size; a parking garage for a plethora of toy cars, trucks, and trains. This is largely thanks to my parents and in-laws, who feel obliged to turn our home into a Toys"R"Us.

But even though they have all these things, what my kids love to play with the most are random objects, such as the aforementioned roadside rocks and defective silverware handles. (Coincidentally, these were the hottest Christmas gifts during the Great Depression.)

My son's "Oink" and "Moo" were originally handles to spoons that I won as part of an ice cream gift basket. He broke the spoon ends off almost immediately, of course, and has been captivated by the animal-shaped handles ever since. Combined with an old silver necklace of my wife's, which he refers to as his "beads", these three objects can keep The Animal busy for hours.

Besides her pet rock, Boogs also has a pet ladybug that she found on a recent weekend getaway. After placing it inside a freezer bag, which she had me blow air into, she showed the bug a movie on her portable, kid-computer-thingamabob, which refers to as her "pooter." Later on we moved the insect into a more comfortable abode—a juice glass with a piece of perforated wax paper rubber-banded to the top. The ladybug has been "sleeping" for several days now, which doesn't seem to worry my daughter in the least.

Oh, and she also likes to play with dental floss.

So you see, folks, you don't have to buy into the crazed consumerism that corporations try to sell us as the "American Dream." If you just let your kids use their imagination, they'll realize that an empty toilet paper roll can be just as fun as a new Xbox 360. Does this mean I'll never let my kids play video games? Of course not. My Atari 2600 is ready and waiting in the basement as soon as they're old enough to operate a joystick.

I wish I could figure out what free, random objects my kids will become enamored with next. That way I could save money on their birthdays or Christmas by getting them a piece of bark, a broken spatula, or maybe even a new pet stink bug.

Lord knows we've got plenty of those.

Daddy Strikes Again

"Hey! Where's Lady?" asks Boogieface, speaking of her pet ladybug, which had been residing inside a juice glass on top of the fireplace mantel. That is, until I threw it out earlier that day.

She hadn't mentioned or even looked at the stupid thing in over a week. Now, as we're entertaining some friends on a Saturday night, she suddenly remembers her six-legged pet and begins to comb the house for it.

"Lady! Laaaaaady!" she calls, doing a room-to-room search. I get a sick feeling in my stomach as I think back to that moment earlier in the day when, just before releasing the bug back into the wild, I debated about first consulting my daughter. Nah, I thought. She'll never miss it.

"Oh, Laaaaaady! Where are you?"

Then again…

"Boogs," I say. "Come here. Daddy has something to tell you." Cassie turns and looks at me, wide-eyed and concerned. I then explain to my daughter how I freed her ladybug earlier in the day while she was napping. "It hadn't had food or water in a week, honey. It was dying." Of course, even if it somehow managed not to be eaten by some winter-starved bird, the bug had most certainly frozen to death by this point.

Cue the tears. My little girl runs to her mother' arms, crushed that her daddy has betrayed her and cast her beloved Lady out in the merciless wilderness, i.e., the backyard. I try to justify my actions, but she is inconsolable.

Cassie jumps in and tries to diffuse the situation. "How about if we leave some bread out on the back porch for it?" she says.

This momentarily calms by hysterical first born. "Yeah!" she says. "And then we can catch her and bring her back inside." And so the two of them head off to the kitchen—my daughter with new-found hope, my wife giving me the familiar what-in-the-world-were-you-thinking look.

Later that evening I am sitting on the living room floor working on my laptop when I notice movement on the carpet. Unbelievably, crawling right next to me is a ladybug! Could it possibly be Lady? Who gives a crap? I'm saved! I immediately scoop it up and seal it inside another juice glass, covering the opening with a piece of wax paper and a rubber band.

The next morning I can't wait to tell my daughter that her beloved Lady has returned. But as I pick up the glass, something is missing: the ladybug! Then I notice that I had failed to properly seal the opening, creating a means of escape.

Daddy strikes again.

Remarkably, Boogieface is disappointed but upbeat about the situation. "Well," she says, "at least it's back inside the house now."

"Yeah!" I say, impressed with her mature optimism. "That's what really matters." I just hope she won't want me to try to find it.

"Let's try to find it!" she says.

Despite a desperate all-morning search, the new Lady is nowhere to be found, and I realize now that I will have to Google "ladybugs for sale" and place my first-ever online insect purchase.

Then, the next morning, my wife discovers a ladybug crawling on the dining room wall. Again, she puts the bug in a glass, this time with some food (a leaf from a house plant and an orange slice) and some water, and makes sure to seal it in. But then Boogieface changes her mind. "I don't want her to be dead," she says. "I want her to sleep on the wall. Then we can find her that way, and she won't die."

How can you argue with that logic?

So what did we learn here? And by "we" I mean "me." We learned that it is never wise to release your child's pet into the wild without their consent.

We also learned that we may need an exterminator.

Barely Surviving at 30,000 Feet

"Look, Daddy: my nuts are getting a little sun!" announces my daughter, loud enough to draw the attention of everyone in the cramped cabin of the DC-10.

We were on a flight to Florida to visit my sister, and Boogieface wanted to show me how she had carefully placed her peanuts on the windowsill next to her, not wanting to eat Delta's generous offering in one fell swoop. Hence the nuts-in-the-sun declaration.

As pleasurable experiences go, flying with young kids ranks right up there with a colonoscopy. It all starts with the preparation, which begins weeks before the actual flight. It's like planning for an expedition to Mt. Everest. You have to make sure to pack for any possible situation, just so you can avoid potential disaster at 30,000 feet.

First you have to pick out and pack the kids' clothes—a difficult job, which, thank goodness, my wife handles. I'm in charge of the Toy Selection Process, which, although more interesting, can be just as tricky. You have to make sure you select toys that a) are lightweight, b) are relatively quiet, and c) will be able to keep the kids' attention for the duration of the flight. For Boogieface, who prefers stuffed animals, this is pretty easy. The Animal, on the other hand, likes to play with small trucks and trains and Matchbox cars, which can create quite a ruckus when smashed together (which they most certainly will be) and which will almost certainly end up on the floor of the plane, where, due to the cramped seating, they will be virtually impossible to pick up again until the flight is over.

Our one must-have travel item is the portable DVD player. My kids immediately become zombies when confronted by glowing rectangles of any kind and will stay completely motionless and quiet as long as they're watching a movie. It's a little scary actually. Sometimes we have to take their pulse just to make sure they're still breathing.

On this particular flight, we also had to bring along a stroller and a car seat, which only enhanced the misery of the experience.

Getting all this gear, plus our carry-on bags and our kids, through the airport is an adventure in itself. Being the closest thing resembling a man in our family, it's usually up to me to do most of the heavy lifting. At one point, while rushing to make our connection, I was carrying a backpack, my daughter's carry-on suitcase, the cumbersome car seat, and Boogieface herself, who was riding on Daddy's shoulders because she was too tired to pull her suitcase anymore. I felt like a Sherpa.

Going through security with kids is where the real fun begins. Suddenly you feel like the guy who snuck 20 items into the 8-items-and-under aisle, while a line of annoyed people impatiently wait for you to check out. It took about 16 of those big plastic bins to cart all of our stuff through the scanner. Then, after we finally made it through, we had to wait for them to check my son's sippy cup for explosive liquids. Little did they know the potentially explosive device *was* my son.

Once you get to the gate, you can just sense the hatred coming at you from all directions. Although they might have oh-your-kids-are-so-cute smiles on their faces, you know what the other passengers are really thinking: *How dare you bring children onto an airplane! Your snot-nosed brats better not disturb me whilst I read my Sky Mall magazine. The nerve!*

As you board the plane, the glares become even more menacing as you try to make your way to the back of the plane down that narrow aisle, your carry-on bags and the car seat coming precariously close to making contact with the oh-so-privileged people in First Class. Those jerks.

On the flight down, my kids were uncharacteristically well-behaved. On the way back, however, we ran into the perfect storm. Our flight was delayed and we found ourselves up in the air right smack in the middle of dinner time with two hungry and tired kids. Boogieface, unbeknownst to me, scarfed down our only form of sustenance: a container of Pepperidge Farm Goldfish crackers. Then the DVD player battery ran out. For the last hour or so, it was everything I could do to keep my napless, ravenous son under control. During the remainder of the flight, he let out a few shockingly loud yelps, as he is wont to do, and he was relentless in kicking the seat in front of him. But other than that, I somehow managed to keep him from eating his tray table until we landed.

Friendly skies, my ass.

Welcome to Hoopie Beach

I am only gone for ten minutes. But in the time it takes me to drive to my sister's house and back to get the beach towels, all hell has broken loose.

"Daddy! Look at me!" my daughter cries out from the shore line, where she is sitting, fully clothed, in the sub-60-degree waters of the Gulf of Mexico. "I'm peeing in the ocean!"

"Welcome to Hoopie Beach," says my sister, resigned to the fact she and my wife have completely lost control of the situation. Just then her two-year-old daughter scampers past us down the beach, sans diaper. I look over to see my son, still soaking-wet from falling into the water, teeth chattering, as he sits in the sand munching on a sand-covered apple slice.

Yeah, this was a great idea.

I've never been much of a beach person. When I was five, my family and I went to Cocoa Beach in Florida during a Disney World vacation, and on our first day the tops of my feet were badly sunburned. For the rest of the week I set up camp underneath a beach umbrella, wearing a hat, t-shirt, and socks, while the rest of my family jumped and frolicked around in the surf.

Strike one.

Years later, I was playing in the shallow waters of Ocean City, Md., when I started having a rather uncomfortable pinching feeling in a certain unmentionable area. It felt like I had fire ants in my bathing suit. The culprit: sea lice. All I remember is darting back to the hotel and jumping into a hot shower as I tried to rid myself of the tiny, crotch-invading critters.

Strike two.

By the time I'd reached college, I'd pretty much had it with the beach. I still went on spring break, but I spent most of the time inside a beach tent, a large cup of Dunkin' Donuts and a *USA Today* in hand. (I was a real party animal.) The one time I dared venture out of my shelter – a mere half hour to toss the Frisbee around with my friend – I ended up getting sun poisoning so bad that the skin on my chest looked like crust bubbles on a pepperoni pizza.

Strike three.

So when my wife and sister suggested we take the kids down to the beach for the afternoon, I was, of course, less than enthusiastic. But then I figured, it's the middle of winter, so the sun shouldn't be too intense. Plus, the water's so cold that we won't have to worry about anyone actually going in. Then, five minutes after we get there, The Animal runs down to the water and falls, fully clothed, into the frigid, salty Gulf. And since we forgot to bring any towels with us, I have to make a run back to the house.

And that brings us back again to Hoopie Beach.

We stick around for another 45 minutes or so, three adults chasing after four very wet, sticky, sandy kids, as the other beach-goers glare at us disapprovingly. Meanwhile, the powdery white sand is finding its way into our lives forever, thanks in part to my son, who still thinks all things are meant to be eaten or thrown.

Did I mention how much I like the beach?

The Craft from Hell

"You guys wanna do a craft?!" my wife says to the kids, just as we finish up another exhausting family dinner.

My children, who, for the last hour or so, have been whining and complaining about their food as if it were cough-syrup-covered cockroaches, suddenly spring to life and yell out in approval.

"YAY! A CRAFT!!!"

Since I already made a date with the sofa, I am stunned and saddened by this unexpected turn of events. Cassie is quite familiar with my facial expressions and senses my lack of enthusiasm. "Oh, com'on," she says. "It will be fun!"

Fun? Happy hour is fun. Going to the movies, fun. Embarking on a complicated construction project with a rambunctious two-year-old and a four-year-old drama queen? Yeah, sounds like a real hoot.

Apparently my wife found a craft in Disney's *FamilyFun Magazine* and then downloaded the directions online. The final product was to be an elaborate cardboard tree house, "perfect for nature-loving peg dolls and fairies," according to the description on the magazine's site. Personally, I've never met a "nature-loving peg doll" and/or fairy.

But then again I'm sort of a homebody.

The craft looks simple enough – an obvious red flag – and so I decide to play along. As I go down to the basement to get some cardboard boxes for cutting, Cass and the kids clear the table to make room for some serious crafting fun.

Fifteen minutes into the project, my hand is already cramping from cutting the four long cardboard pieces for the trunk of the tree house.

I'm a writer, for cryin' out loud. I'm not used to this type of physical labor. It's also around this time that Boogieface decides that she's had enough "fun" and leaves to go play with some real, already assembled, store-bought toys. The Animal is nowhere to be found. He was out before we even started cutting. Smart kid.

An hour in we are still nowhere near completion, and my dining room looks like the inside of a dumpster. Then, as we try to start assembling the tree house, we realize that we cut out the main trunk pieces backwards, and they won't fit together properly. As a result, the tree house looks more like a sorry excuse for a rocket ship.

"YEAH!" says Boogieface, her interest in the project renewed. "A rocket ship!" So now we're building the world's very first wood-paneled rocket ship.

By the time we finally finish (over two hours later!) it's way past the kids' bedtime, my right hand has become a useless claw, and our tree house/rocket ship, which is held together with duct tape, looks neither like a tree house nor a rocket ship. Regardless, the kids love it. That is, they love it for the remaining 15 minutes they're awake. After that night, they never actually play with the cardboard monstrosity again.

We keep the deformed tree house/rocket ship around the house for a couple more weeks, solely out of principle, occasionally patching it with more duct tape as needed. After all, I sacrificed over two hours of my life making that damned thing. And I have the claw-hand to prove it.

Finally, unable to bear the sight of it any longer, I take the Craft from Hell out behind the woodshed and put it out of its misery. Hopefully my wife will remember this little crafting catastrophe and not subject us to similar "fun" projects in the future.

Rest in peace, deformed cardboard tree house/rocket ship. We barely knew ye.

Animalistic Behavior

The crash was tremendous. It sounded like the china cabinet had fallen over. Then I remembered that we don't have a china cabinet.

I was sitting behind my desk in the den talking to Boogieface when it happened. First I heard a dragging sound. Then came the crash, followed by my son's screeching. I jumped up and followed the sound of his cries, my daughter trailing close behind.

When I turned the corner of the kitchen, I found my son sprawled out on what appeared to be a bed of ice. But it wasn't ice. It was shattered glass from the door of the oven. I immediately scooped up my little guy and dusted off the little flecks of glass that covered his arms, checking for any cuts. Luckily he was fine. He was more scared than anything.

Once I determined he was OK, I began to piece together the clues of the crime scene using the detective skills I acquired at a young age from reading Hardy Boys mysteries.

From what I could surmise, The Animal spied a sippy cup on the kitchen counter. He then went to the dining room to retrieve his sister's high chair, which he dragged into the kitchen and climbed on top to try to grab the cup. As he reached out for his prize, the chair must have slipped out from underneath him, sending him falling toward the floor. On the way down, his head, or possibly the sippy cup made contact with the oven door, shattering the outer layer of glass.

Of course, this is just a guess at what happened. As the shards of glass continued to crackle and pop all over the floor like a bowl of Rice Krispies, I decided to ask my son for an explanation, which he provided. Sort of:

"I was falling in the cup, and it keep going in the cup. I twying to get one cup. It A-B-C cup. I keep falling, I keep falling. It keep going in that cup."

That certainly cleared things up.

He seemed pretty shaken up about the whole thing, so I asked him once more if he was OK.

"Yeah. It was not falling. It was falling on that oven. It was keep going in that oven."

At least he was speaking clearly, which ruled out a concussion.

I'm not sure if I'll ever get used to having a boy. The kid's been around for over two years now and I'm still not accustomed to his adventurous nature. Boogieface never attempted anything like this. We didn't even have to gate the stairs for her; she just wasn't interested.

The Animal, on the other hand, is constantly building makeshift ladders in order to reach things we try to put out of his reach. And if we forget to secure the gate at the bottom of the staircase, he immediately senses it and makes a mad dash up the steps, where he can then raid his sister's bedroom or make for the bathroom and clean his teeth with the toilet brush.

For the next half hour or so, my wife and I scoured the floor for the tiny shards of glass that were scattered throughout the kitchen. Meanwhile, my daughter stood in the doorway and worked as a spotter.

"There's another piece of ice!" she said, still not grasping what had just happened.

"It's not ice," I corrected her. "It's broken glass."

"Look, Daddy, more ice—over there!"

"Thanks, Boogs."

Once we got all the "ice" cleaned up, I called the local appliance store to see just how much this little sippy cup fiasco was going to cost us. It turns out our oven is so old that it might cost as much to replace the glass as it would to buy a brand new oven. Splendid.

But of course, boys will be boys, and accidents happen. The important thing is that my son wasn't seriously injured.

As for the oven, I'm not really worried about the money. We'll just take it out of his college savings.

BFFs (Best Frenemies Forever)

On the cuteness meter, few things register as high as two adorable little four-year-old cousins playing dolls together. It really warms the heart.

"Her's being nasty!"

"Nuh uh! She has my favorite baby doll and she's not sharing!"

"I'm not playing with you anymore!"

"Well, I'm not playing with you ever again! So there!"

Isn't that sweet?

Every once in a while, when my wife and sister-in-law head out to the gym or maybe the store, I have the privilege of watching my kids and my niece for a few hours. It sounds simple enough. All I have to do is let the little munchkins run around and play while I pour myself a cup of coffee and grab a good book, checking up on the them periodically, just to make sure they're not cutting each other's hair or feeding LEGOs to the garbage disposal.

Of course, it's never that simple.

As I curl up on the sofa with my book, the girls start playing this make-believe game they call "Happy Family," where one is the "mom", another is the "kid", and my son, fittingly, plays the part of "the dog."

Just minutes into their game, however, their happy little family transforms into a dysfunctional one, as the girls begin to antagonize each other. First comes the tattling. "She's not sharing!" or "Her's not being nice!" or "She just said a bad word!" By this time The Animal has lost interest in the game and crawls off to go find something to destroy.

At this point I start to feel the blood begin to bubble inside my veins. I try to remain calm, however, and refuse to let them get to me. "I don't want to hear about it," I say, washing my hands of the situation. "Go figure it out yourselves." My wife first shared with me this brilliant style of parenting, which not only teaches your children how to resolve their own issues but which also sends them back to whence they came with a puzzled look on their face. It's really quite satisfying.

But of course, this is only a temporary solution. Minutes later another one comes running in to tell you that the other just called her a "poopie head."

Soon my patience runs out and I begin to make bold declarations: "That's it!" I declare. "Unless someone is bleeding to death, I don't want to hear about it! Do you understand me? NOW GO HAVE FUN!"

By this time I've given up on my book and begin to stare out the window, longingly, like an inmate on Rikers.

Once they realize they can't tattle anymore, the girls resort to something more sinister: spite. My daughter and my niece are both masters of malice, and each knows exactly how to push the other's buttons.

For example, this one time they were fighting over the same coloring book page, so I jumped in to resolve the dispute. "This is your side," I said to one, drawing a line down the center of the page, "and this side is yours." Problem solved. Or so I thought. Immediately they both started coloring as close to the center as possible, their elbows crossing the line of demarcation and colliding with each other's Crayola.

"Her is getting in my way!"

"Know I'm not! She isn't staying on her side!"

It's usually around this time that I go and pour myself a stiff drink. A double. Meanwhile The Animal is off somewhere mutilating a book or guzzling sour milk from some long-forgotten sippy cup.

But as long as he's not bothering me, I really don't care.

The Art of Deception

When I was a kid my father would always tell us that he could fly. And we believed him.

Although my sisters and I never actually saw him take wing, he'd demonstrate his flying technique to us by taking deep breaths and moving his arms up and down in a flapping motion. According to him, he'd start at the top of the driveway and run down the long strip of grass in our front yard before lifting off like a mallard from the water. Or at least that's how I always imagined it.

Dad also had us convinced that we had wombats living in our woods. Every Saturday morning, while my sisters and I zoned out to Looney Tunes on the old wood-paneled Zenith, he would head into my bedroom, look out the window and proclaim in a loud and excited voice, "Hey, kids…LOOK! There's a wombat in the backyard!" Our house was surrounded on three sides by woods, and we were used to seeing plenty of wildlife—deer, rabbits, raccoons, groundhogs, chipmunks (a.k.a., Grinnies), and the occasional fox. But never wombats. Heck, I didn't even know what a wombat was. (This was pre-Google, for all you youngsters out there.) So whenever my dad would say the word "wombat", we'd snap out of our TV daze and sprint to the bedroom, hoping to catch a glimpse of the mysterious beast.

But alas, just as we'd clamber up onto the top bunk and peer out the window, Dad would claim that the wombat had slipped back into the shadows of the forest. "Shoot!" he'd say. "You just missed it."

This went on for years. Literally. And although I had my doubts, I could never find enough evidence to prove that my father was lying to us. He never came out and admitted it either, even when we were old enough to know that humans were incapable of unassisted flight and that wombats were only found "Down Under." After all those years, I think he actually believed it himself.

Now that I'm a father, I too have discovered the fun of lying to your children. It's truly one of the great joys of parenthood.

For example, I've convinced both of my kids that they possess Jedi-like powers and that they can roll down their backseat window simply by pointing at it and making a quick "CHOO!" sound. Watching through the rearview mirror, I secretly ready my hand on the window control buttons on my door. Then, as they raise their finger towards the glass and make the special sound – PRESTO! – the window magically goes down.

"I DID IT!" exclaims my son, beaming from ear to ear. Meanwhile, Boogieface toys with him, using her own magic powers to roll his window back up.

Another one of my favorites is the old pull-something-out-of-the-ear trick. I've done this to my daughter dozens of times with coins, rings, pieces of candy, etc. The thing is, now any time we misplace something, she calls upon me to use my special power. "Daddy," she says, "I can't find my dolly. Check in my ear."

Remote controls can be a lot of fun, too. Just by secretly concealing the remote in my pocket, I've convinced my daughter that she can change the stations on my shelf radio simply by pointing at it and saying "Hi-ya!" (She came up with the karate sound on her own.) Strangely, it only works when Daddy is in the room. But that doesn't seem to bother her.

Cass and I actually struggle with certain untruths, like whether or not we should tell our kids the real deal about Santa and the Easter Bunny. After all, we don't want to lose their trust in us. But for some reason, I have no problem whatsoever making them believe that they can move inanimate objects just by waving their hand like Obi-Wan Kenobi.

Sometimes I actually lie in order to protect them, like when I tell them there's a dragon chained up in the basement, just so they won't try to descend the stairs. Am I risking frightening them by telling them this? Maybe. But in my experience, "Watch out for the dragon!" is much more effective than "Because I said so!"

So I guess as long as they'll believe me, I'll keep telling tall tales to my kids. It's harmless fun, really. Besides, I know it won't be long before they smarten up and realize that Daddy is full of you-know-what.

And when that happens, I'll just focus all my energy on embarrassing them. Which I'm sure is just as fun.

To Pre-School—and Beyond!

"Let's play spaceship!" Boogieface says to me from the back seat, as we negotiate the rush-hour traffic on the way to pre-school. "You be Buzz, I'll be Jessie, and Tinkerbell will be Tinkerbell."

It's 7:30 in the morning. Before my first cup of coffee. At this hour I'd prefer to ease into the day with a little sports talk radio than engage in a spirited game of make-believe. But I have a hard time saying no to my daughter, so I play along. At least she didn't ask me to play that maddening kiddie music CD for the gazillionth time.

Both of my kids are obsessed with the "Toy Story" movies, those Disney-Pixar cash cows about toys that come alive when no one is around. My son actually wakes up reciting lines from the films; he's got Buzz Lightyear on the brain. This particular morning Boogs has brought her new Tinkerbell doll into the mix, too, making it sort of a Disney reunion.

As we cruise down main street, I channel my inner Tim Allen: "Tooooooo infinity...and beyond!"

My daughter joins in. "Watch out for the aliens!"

"What aliens? Where?"

"Right there, Daddy...I mean, Buzz. The cars—they're all aliens! Get them with your shooter!"

I press the imaginary button on my right arm and blast away at the "aliens" all around us. "Whew! I think I got them all," I say. Meanwhile, other drivers stare at me like I'm a lunatic.

"Woody! Look out—Zurg's on the roof!!"

"Woody?" I say. "I thought I was Buzz?"

"No, you're Woody now. Buzz is back at home with Mommy." My daughter's imagination is quite flexible.

"Oh. But I don't have a shooter like Buzz," I say, in my best Tom Hanks voice, which sounds nothing like Tom Hanks. "What should I do?"

"Don't worry," she says, "Tinkerbell has a shooter, and she already got Zurg!

"Nice shootin', Tinkerbell!" Three words I never thought I'd say.

"And I have a shooter, too—and it shoots water!"

"Oh, good!" I say. "I feel so much better now." At this point I try to stay quiet for a few seconds to see if maybe we can take a little break from make-believe, which can be surprisingly rigorous first thing in the morning.

But my little girl is just getting warmed up. "BUZZ!" she yells out. "Get ready for blast off!"

"Wait a second…I thought you said Buzz was at home with Mommy and that I was Woody now?"

"You can be Woody AND Buzz," she replies. "Now get ready for blast off! Five…four…three…two…one…BLAST OFF!"

I jump on the accelerator, taking my Hyundai from 30 to 35 m.p.h. in a mere two seconds flat before decelerating back down to 30 again. It's a high-performance vehicle.

"Go faster, Daddy…I mean, Buzz!"

"I can't fly the spaceship too fast in town, honey. The space police will come after us."

"More aliens! Get them with your shooter!" This goes on the entire 15 minutes or so to pre-school.

Flash-forward to later that afternoon when I pick her up on the way home from work. After a long day at the office, I'm really not in the mood for improvisation. So I try to strike up some easy conversation to distract her. "So…how was school today, honey?"

But Boogs has other plans. "Daddy," she says, "you be Woody, I'll be Jesse, and Tinkerbell will be Tinkerbell."

And so, we blast off again—tooooooo infinity…and beyond! And by that I mean our house.

Suburban Shark Attacks and Things That Go Thump in the Night

First came a loud thump. Then the crying. We had just arrived at our friends' rental house for a relaxing weekend getaway. And since it was well past the kiddos' bedtime, I was upstairs frantically trying to set up the pack 'n play, dreams of Cabernet dancing in my head.

I almost had the bed all set up, when my wife called out to me to come downstairs because our son had fallen.

So what? I thought. The boy falls all the time. Give him a few seconds and he'll be back to his normal boisterous, destructive self.

But when I got downstairs, it was worse than I imagined. Apparently he had fallen backwards from the dining room table, and when his head hit the floor he bit all the way through the skin below his bottom lip. Yikes.

I moved in for a closer look as The Animal wailed away. "This is going to need stitches," I determined, based on the comprehensive medical training I received as an English major.

So once again we loaded the kids into the family truckster and headed off to the closest Med-Express—9 miles back the way we had just come. The Cabernet would have to wait until…um…I mean, hopefully my son would be OK.

Luckily, the doctor said stitches weren't necessary. But she did say that he would probably end up with a scar, which obviously upset my wife. "Don't worry," I said, "Tina Fey has a scar, and look how it's worked out for her!"

Back when I was a kid I fell all the time; I had a real knack for it. My knees were perpetually scabbed from always crashing on my bike and falling off of my skateboard. One time I actually managed to fall *up* a set of cement stairs and ended up with one heck of a goose egg and a matching set of shiners. I also fell down the cellar steps a lot. My mom says I fell so many times that she was worried I'd end up with brain damage when I grew up. The verdict's still out on that one.

Cass and I do our best to keep our kids safe and scar-free, but it seems like disaster always strikes when you least expect it.

For example, on a recent Saturday morning, we decided to take a little walk around town. The Animal was secure in his stroller, and Boogieface was in her usual spot, sitting on top near the handle, where she's sat a million times before without incident. The sun was out, a cool breeze was at our backs, and all was right with the world.

Just then the front wheel caught the edge of the curb, bringing the stroller to an abrupt halt. Boogs went flying forward and landed on the back of her brother's head, driving his face down into the cup holder. Luckily I caught a hold of her dress before she could fall to the street. The Animal wasn't so lucky. Pinned beneath his sister, his face had been driven into the dorsal fin of his plastic toy shark. Now he had another bloody gash on his face to match the one that had just about healed underneath his lip.

So much for the Parents of the Year award.

Could we have prevented my son from falling off the table and biting through his lip? Maybe. Could we have foreseen the Great Stroller Catastrophe? Probably. But, as they say, [bleep] happens—especially when kids are involved. All you can do is be vigilant, keep your eyes peeled for possible hazards, and have your smartphone handy so you can locate the nearest emergency room.

Afterward you can go off and drown your parental guilt with a couple glasses of wine. Which always makes me feel better.

A Memorable Weekend

Despite my high hopes, nothing really extraordinary happened during our little Memorial Day weekend road trip. No ghastly injuries. No demonic possessions. Darn.

Regardless, I thought I'd share some of the highlights:

Around noon on Saturday, we arrived in the tiny hamlet of Chagrin Falls, Ohio, which was quite lively due to its annual Blossom Time Festival. After perusing some of the stores and checking out the waterfall, we stopped at the Popcorn Shop Factory for some much-needed sustenance: ice cream for the kids and iced coffee for Dad.

I wanted to continue strolling around town, but the kids fell victim to the Siren call of the local carnival. So off we went to pay way too much to ride a bunch of rickety deathtraps and win some worthless tchotchkes. As the kiddos stood in line to risk their lives, I got lost in a Coney Island dog.

Over at Chuck's Fine Wines, my son helped me pick out a nice bottle for the evening. "How 'bout da one with da woof?" he suggested, pointing to a bottle with a wolf on the label. It also had a $69.95 price tag on it. I decided to go with the $12.95 bottle—my favorite vintage.

Next we dined at a much-too-high-end-for-people-with-young-kids type restaurant. Since it was relatively empty at the time, we decided to risk it all for some good sushi. I ordered a Smutty Nose Old Dog Brown Ale, which was apropos, since I had been battling seasonal allergies all day. Meanwhile Boogieface played drums with her chopsticks as The Animal smashed his die-cast cars together again and again. Of course neither of them would eat anything off of the menu. Yet somehow we managed to spend $75 smackers.

Back outside, we stumbled upon a whole line of vendors selling an array of festival foods at much more reasonable prices. Sure, a corn dog isn't seared ahi, but it isn't $5 a bite either. Their stomachs empty from their sushi boycott, the kids devoured a mountainous helping of flavored ice.

Next we high-tailed it over to the local high school to wait over an hour to watch a hot-air balloon launch that, much to our "Chagrin" (sorry) never happened, due to the blustery 3-mph winds.

Back at the hotel, the kids fell asleep in minutes, worn out from a long day of spending our money. I too was exhausted, but I dug deep and mustered the strength to drink a few glasses of Horse Haven Hills Cab, while the soothing sounds of a classic-rock cover band rattled the hotel windows from a bar across the street.

I woke up early Sunday morning with Boogs and vegged on the couch as she watched something hideous on Nickelodeon. Then, after blowing my nose seventeen times, me and my sand-filled eyes went downstairs and brought back some quasi-Cheerios type cereal for the kids, which, of course, they immediately rejected. Minutes later, Cassie went down and returned with some sausage, fruit, and waffles for the kids and one of those What-the-heck-were-you-thinking? looks for me.

After splashing around in the hotel's petri-dish of a swimming pool, we headed off one of those "family fun" places that offer tons of ways for you to flush your hard-earned cash down the drain. It cost $22.50 just for the four of us to roller skate. Two minutes in, my son abruptly quit, wanting instead to go play on the Big Climbing Contraption Thingamabob, a.k.a., the Germ Factory.

All the fun and microbes you can enjoy for $6 bucks!

On the way home, we stopped for lunch at a much more kid-appropriate establishment in Hudson. Of course, the little buggers still wouldn't eat. But I was quite pleased with my Dark Horse Lager and meatloaf sliders.

If you couldn't tell, the theme for the weekend was "Healthy Eating."

Finally, Memorial Day arrived. All week long Boogs had been so excited to decorate her bike and ride it in the annual parade in town. However, on the way to the parade, just half way up the block, she said she didn't want to ride in it after all. Then she flat refused to even push her bike and began crying hysterically. She ended up watching the parade from inside Cafe Kolache, mostly because she was terrified of the fire trucks' sirens, which they didn't even end up using. The Animal, on the other hand, wowed the crowd as he cruised around on his new balance bike, flirting with girls like a lone wolf on a Harley.

So with the crazy allergies, the unforeseen expenses, minor mishaps and breakdowns, and the new bevy of microorganisms we now host in our bowels, I guess it was a pretty memorable weekend after all.

And we have a big, pink, $5 dollar plastic dolphin – a.k.a., Squeaky Pinkish – to remind us of it, lest we forget.

A Family Tradition

"Com'on, honey…you can do it! I know you can. We're almost there…just one more push…"

"I caaaan't…I'm too tired!"

"Yes you can! You're being so brave! Com'on…just one more big push—I promise!"

There are moments in your life that you'll never forget; ones that are so dramatic, so emotional, that they become permanently embedded in your memory. Like when your children are born.

Or that time when you spent an hour and a half in the bathroom with your bawling four-year-old, as you coached her through a successful and freakishly large bowel movement.

Unfortunately, the latter has become commonplace in our house. I'm not sure if it's hereditary or a major lack of fiber in her diet, but Boogieface has forced me to hone my plumbing abilities in the past couple of years. If the plunger was a musical instrument, I'd be a virtuoso.

During these moments, I'm reminded of this one time when I was around six or seven years old. My grandparents were babysitting my sisters and me, when I was struck with a terrible stomachache. Such abdominal pains were common for me, since I'd do everything in my power to put off going No. 2. Of course, after about a week of squinching, I'd be more backed up than the DMV on a Saturday morning.

My grandmother, however, was a firm believer in maintaining a healthy bowel, and she was determined to end my suffering. She immediately took me to the bathroom and sat me on the "commode", as she called it. Then, the devoted Catholic that she was, she knelt before me and began to pray the Rosary, beseeching the Almighty to relieve me of my misery.

Despite my grandmother's pleas, an hour or so went by with no progress. Apparently the Good Lord had more important matters to attend to. But Grandma was not deterred. While continuing to pray, she resorted to Plan B: the dreaded enema. I have no words to describe that experience, so I'll just leave it to your imagination. (You're welcome.)

Another hour or so went by with more Rosaries and more enemas. By this time I was utterly exhausted and more than ready to throw in the towel. But Grandma was steadfast in her mission, and she kept me there as long as it took, saying the Hail Mary and Our Father over and over.

Finally, when it was all over, I stumbled to my bed, sweaty and completely pooped, so to speak. Although it was only 7 p.m., I slept straight through 'til 10 o'clock the next morning, my body needing to recuperate from the physically and mentally taxing experience.

During my daughter's most recent bathroom marathon, I didn't say the Rosary or resort to the dreaded Plan B. But I did say a few prayers during the process. I even asked Grandma, wherever she was, to use her good standing with the Almighty and ask him to give my baby girl a break, as long as He wasn't off saving some shipwrecked sailors, smiting the wicked, or helping Tim Tebow throw a touchdown.

Eventually my little girl was relieved of her burden and bouncing around the house like a normal four-year-old again. Meanwhile I was back at work with the plunger, working my magic.

That's Not Water!

I've always known it was coming. Like a slowly approaching storm, far off on the horizon. Ominous. Inevitable. I'm talking, of course, of the day when we'd have to start potty training my son.

Boogieface, you see, was no walk in the park. We started when she was 17 months old and didn't finish until more than a year later, thanks to a three-month period when she decided that she preferred the convenience of diapers after all, and went on a potty boycott.

We decided to wait a little longer with The Animal, for various reasons. For one, his "hardware" is a little more complicated. Secondly, he's more Tasmanian devil than toddler. But when he started waking up with a dry diaper, we begrudgingly admitted it was time. So I dragged the dusty old Elmo potty up from the basement, and so began the training.

Our first attempt to civilize our young man was relatively successful. It was a challenge, however, just keeping him on the potty until nature took its course. Then, after reading every book in the house to him and entertaining him with every toy I could find, his patience had worn thin. I actually had to physically hold him down as I pleaded with him to stay put. Finally, nearly two hours in—Hallelujah!—we had pee.

Since that first marathon struggle, it really hasn't been too bad. Oh, he puts up a fight at first. But then we just bribe him with M&Ms, and suddenly it's Niagara Falls. Pavlov would be proud.

Surprisingly, he has been relatively cooperative when we go out to eat. However, the strange, horseshoe-shaped toilet seats you sometimes find in public bathrooms can leave a parent dangerously unprotected from a boy's unpredictable stream, which can make for a shameful, soggy walk back to your table.

Funny thing is, every time he's finished doing his business, he immediately stands up, points to the potty and says, "Look, Daddy…water!" My wife and I try to make it very clear that the liquid in the potty is *not* water. This is the kid, after all, who licked the bottom of his shoe, which had been resting in the street gutter, just to quench his thirst. This is the kid who, whenever we give him a shower, lies down flat on the floor to suck the warm, filthy water into his mouth. We understand that he has a drinking problem, and we're terrified that we'll walk in to the bathroom one day to find him slurping down the freshly squeezed contents of his red-plastic bedpan.

One thing I'm looking forward to, personally, is teaching my boy about the joys of peeing outside. There's nothing quite like "watering" the flower garden late at night, beneath a clear, moonlit sky. It's a liberating experience and one of the greatest gifts a father can share with his son.

So despite getting peed on daily and living in fear of the dreaded public accident, my wife and I both understand that if we just put in a couple months of hard work, we can be free from diapers forever and be able to use that money for more important things.

Like red wine and babysitters.

Five Years In

"Daddy…" she says to me, on the eve of her birthday, "When I turn five I'm gonna pretend I'm still four, 'cause I like being four and I don't want to get any bigger."

[Sigh.]

It's hard to believe I've been a dad for five years now. Seems more like twenty. Don't get me wrong, it's been the best five years of my life. I just can't remember what life was like without kids. Seriously. I have some hazy memories of Friday night Tequila Clubs and sleeping in past 8 a.m. on Saturday mornings; of having something called "free time" and sitting on bar stools for hours without a care in the world. But those days more like a dream than anything.

Now, in addition to myself, I'm responsible for the well-being of two other human beings. Now "going out" means walking to the supermarket to pick up some milk. And it's become second nature to say things like "Hey! We don't hit our sister!" and "Get your shoe out of your mouth!"

What a difference five years makes.

For her birthday all Boogieface wanted was to go to the zoo and pet the stingrays. I remember the first time we did this. You'll understand if I was a little wary about letting my then 3-year-old daughter reach out and pet the creature that tragically ended the life of Steve Irwin, a man who captured crocodiles and poisonous snakes for a living—with his bare hands.

But of course everything went fine. The only sting came when I paid $20 for a new purple stuffed stingray toy. Ouch.

So I left work a little early and met up with Cass and the kids and we sped to the city, trying to get to the zoo before they closed the gates at 4 p.m. Thanks to Pittsburgh's perpetual road construction, we barely made it. Then the charming ticket booth attendant had us pay full price—$52 dollars, plus another $8 for a Jeep-style stroller/wagon do-hickie. My now empty wallet did made it a little easier, though, to push the kids through the surprisingly hilly zoo as we made a bee-line for the aquarium.

Boogs was once again thrilled to touch the alien-like rays, or "swimmies" as she calls them. After that we spent the remaining 40 minutes or so express touring of the rest of the zoo, my daughter's birthday wish fulfilled.

"Look, guys—a giraffe!"

"Where, Daddy?"

"Too late! We have to get to the sea lions before they lock us in here!"

Later on we ate at the Spaghetti Warehouse, just as we had last year, so that Boogieface could have her beloved "sketties and meatballs." It was against our latest family nutritional plan, but on birthdays my rule is that all rules are off.

While we waited for our food, we gave my daughter a few presents, one of which was my old iPod Shuffle, pre-loaded with Adele, Five For Fighting, The Black Eyed Peas, and some of her other favorite artists. It was her first "big girl" present. And although it thrilled me to see her light up as the music coursed through her new ear-buds, I thought I caught a glimpse of my future teenager drowning out Mom and Dad just as I used to back in the day with my Sony Walkman. That alone was enough to make me order a second glass of Cabernet.

So, yeah, five is a big milestone for sure, but I'm OK with it. Really. I'd love it if she could stay this age forever, so sweet, so innocent. Then again, part of me is also excited to watch her grow and learn and become a strong, smart, beautiful young woman.

Besides, I hear five is the new three anyway. So there's no need to panic just yet.

An Open Letter to Future Me

Dear Future Me,

I hope all is well with you.

Things are just dandy here. But, of course, you already knew that.

I know you're busy with book-signing tours, television interviews, and counting your piles of money, so I won't take up too much of your time. But I wanted to talk to you about something…

Now that the kids are all grown up and the nest is empty, so to speak, you may be thinking wistfully of the past. You've probably even been longing for the days when the kids were much younger. After all, like you keep telling yourself, those were the best days of your life.

Heck, I bet you've even turned into one of those people who go around telling parents of young children how "It all goes so fast!" and to "Enjoy this time because, before you know it they'll be all grown up."

Since your then is my now, and since your memory has been clouded by years of drinking too much cheap Cabernet, let me clarify something about the past: It wasn't as great as you remember.

Oh, don't get me wrong, I love my (your) kids more than anything in the world, as we both know, and I think that they are so incredibly cute and fun at this age. Get this: They actually enjoy being around me, and they still think I know everything. Ha! Remember those days? Probably not. Again, the Cabernet.

But over the years your aging brain has played a trick on you. It has allowed you to forget just how mentally and physically exhausted you were during this time of your life. Believe me—you're pooped.

Oh, com'on, you say, I wasn't that tired.

Yes, Future Me. Yes you were.

Unless I'm at the office or asleep or asleep at the office, every second of my (your) life revolves around those little buggers. I'm constantly dressing them, undressing them, bathing them, feeding them, begging them to eat something—anything, putting them in Timeout every five seconds; picking toys off the floor in the living room, the dining room, the bathroom, the kitchen, the laundry room, the bedroom, the front yard, the back yard, the neighbor's yard; packing a bag of toys to keep them busy at the restaurant, picking toys up off of the floor at the restaurant, cleaning up the mess on the floor at the restaurant, telling him not to eat that piece of food on the floor at the restaurant, buckling them into their car seats, taking them out of their car seats, telling her to stop teasing him, telling him to stop hitting her, brushing her hair, brushing his teeth, wiping their noses, wiping their…well, you know, reading them a book, reading them another book, putting them to bed, taking them out of bed to go to the potty, putting them back in bed, coming back upstairs to get them a drink of water…and so many other things that I can't think of right now because, frankly, I'm just too tired.

And lest you forget, Future Me, your only real free time was after they finally went to bed. By that time you were so beat that it was a struggle just to stay up past 9 o'clock. And "free" is a misnomer, because you were actually trapped in the house until you left for work the next morning, when it all started over again.

But I bet you don't remember any of that, do you? You only remember the really good parts, like playing tents or hide-and-seek in the living room, secretly listening to her play school with her stuffed animals, watching him play with your old Matchbox cars, giving them horsey rides around the living room, pushing him on the swing at the park, pretending to eat the pretend cake she made you in the sandbox, hearing them say "DADDY!" as they raced to hug you when you got home from work, holding hands with her as you skipped down the sidewalk, pushing him in his stroller as he pointed out the squirrels, hearing them laugh as you tickled them in their car seats, listening to them sing along to the radio in the back of the car, bouncing him on your shoulders as you walked up-street for ice cream, reading them bedtime stories as they clutched their blankies, holding him close before placing him in his crib for the night, kissing her goodnight as you tucked her in to bed…

You know what, Future Me? Maybe you're right after all. This really is a wonderful time. Maybe the best.

Forget all that stuff I said about how hard things were. (Oh, that's right…you already did.)

I'll check back in when they're teenagers. Hopefully we made it through alive.

Take care,
Past You

PS: College wasn't that great either. (Yeah it was.)

Surviving Family Time

Back in the old days, extended families would live together under the same roof. Grandparents, grandchildren, sisters, brothers, fathers, mothers, aunts, uncles, and cousins would all shack up in one house, sharing resources and, more important, the adventures and blessings of everyday life.

Which explains why the average life expectancy was so much shorter back then.

Over the past two weeks, we shared our home with my younger sister, her husband, and their three adorable daughters – ages 3, 18 months, and 6 months – while they were in town for a visit. Add in my two little ones, and that makes five little munchkins who were running rampant throughout my home from dusk to dawn.

I don't know how I made it out alive.

My house is large, square-footage-wise, but the extra space is mostly vertical, thanks to the high ceilings. This would be helpful if we were housing, say...an NBA team. It is of no benefit, however, when your roomers are less than 3 feet tall.

Words can't describe the amount of devastation five young children can inflict on one's home. Imagine coating every surface on the inside of your house with a layer of honey – your furniture, your walls, your television, etc. – and then inviting a family of ravenous black bear in to have at it. When it's all said and done, everything is sticky, broken, and in complete disarray.

It's sorta like that.

Oh, com'on, you say. They're just children! And little ones at that. How destructive could they be? Believe me, they can do some damage. Don't let their size fool you. Have you ever seen what a colony of army ants can do when they get organized? I rest my case.

I have to be fair to my 6-month-old niece, though. The sweet little angel's not even crawling yet and, therefore, didn't really contribute much to the craziness. Then again, she didn't help much, either.

Dinnertime and bedtime, of course, were the most challenging. I've documented in the past just how difficult it can be to get just my two children to eat dinner. Throw another three into the mix and it's absolute mayhem. Every evening I inhaled my meal as fast as possible, just to get out of the way of the flying food and spilt milk. My poor wife and sister, on the other hand, would go days without eating. They were too busy cooking, cutting, spooning, cleaning, wiping, and refilling.

Nighttime was a whole 'nother ball of wax. Fortunately my children have reached the age where bedtime is reasonably routine. My sister's kids, however, are still at that age where bedtime can be a precarious situation.

Each night while my sister fed the baby, my brother-in-law focused on getting the other two girls to bed. Taking one of his daughters, he'd ascend the stairs to the bedroom, only to return an hour or so later, frustrated and visibly spent. Then he'd take the other one up for round two. Some nights he'd come back; others he'd mysteriously disappear, only to resurface the next morning.

This chaotic atmosphere left little time for cleaning, as you can imagine. Not that we didn't try. In the past two weeks we did 30 loads of dishes, 18 loads of laundry, swept the dining room floor 47 times, cleaned up 23 spills, and picked up the same toys over and over again continuously for 252 hours straight, just to keep from being buried alive.

OK, maybe I'm being a little melodramatic. I have to admit that, despite the mess and the madness, it was really wonderful to spend so much time with family. After all, the mess is temporary, but the memories will last forever. I guess I just need to learn to relax and to enjoy it.

Only next time they come for a visit, I think we'll all enjoy it together over in their suite at the Holiday Inn.

Pining For Christmas

This year we wanted to start a new Christmas tradition with my kids, something we could enjoy together during this special season as we give thanks for our blessings and celebrate the birth of our Lord.

So we decided to go out and kill a perfectly good tree.

I grew up with one of those fake plastic trees and, honestly, I was fine with it. You really couldn't see the tree anyway, buried beneath the ton of tinsel that my mother would meticulously place, piece by piece, on every single fake branch.

I used to love to gaze up at that shimmering plastic pine and bask in the glow of those big old-fashioned lights that would bathe the room in a soft, multi-color glow, and that would actually last more than one year, unlike today's cheapy, made-to-self-destruct-after-one-use lights.

My wife and I have had fake tree ever since we were married 10 years ago, and it has served us well. I actually keep it set up year-round in the basement so that I can just carry it upstairs – scraping the paint from the walls as I go – and plop it in the corner of the living room. That way I avoid spending hours trying to figure out how to assemble it.

This year we thought it would be a little more fun to go out and get a real tree. Not only would it give our home that wonderful pine-fresh smell, but after Christmas, instead of hauling it back down to the basement, I could just drag it out to the curb and let the Borough deal with it. And what's more American than a disposable tree!

So on a recent wintry morning, we packed into the car and headed out to a local Christmas tree farm. The kids were buzzing with excitement when we arrived, and I knew right away that this was going to be a cherished new annual tradition. Then, five seconds out of the car, my son reached down to the ground to grab some snow to eat and ended up with a mouthful of dirt and pine needles. Let the memory-making begin!

We had heard that the best type of tree to get is a Frasier Fir because supposedly it sheds the least amount of needles. So we asked one of the employees to point us in the right direction. "We can't grow them Frasiers up 'ere," said the kind young man, a wad of tobacco tucked firmly in cheek. "What you want is a Douglas Fir. Just head down that-a-way. Can't miss'em."

So I grabbed a tree cart, the kids hopped on, and we headed off into the manmade forest.

Halfway down the trail my son fell off the cart, and I dragged him in the snow for a bit before my daughter alerted me to the situation. Luckily, the little guy was fine. A little dirt in his mouth, but that was nothing new.

After about 15 minutes of comparing the virtues of various trees, we finally found the perfect specimen—a majestic, 8-foot Douglas Fir with a nice full shape and, more important, no signs of bird nests or stink bugs. Next I did my best lumberjack impersonation as the kiddos went off looking for more dirty snow to eat. Then we towed the tree back up the hill, where the Carhartt crew bundled it up as I went inside to buy a stand that cost nearly as much as the tree itself.

Although I still feel a little remorseful about chopping it down, I really do like the way the decorated tree corpse looks in the corner of our living room. Sure, maybe we have to pick up the occasional pine needle and remember to water it every so often, but there's just something so special about a real tree.

Dead and lifeless, though it may be.

The Force is Strong with This One

A few weeks ago, my wife asked The Animal what kind of birthday party he wanted to have, because, you know, you can't just have a normal birthday party anymore. I think there's a law or something.

"A fire-fire party!" he said, emphatically. [Translation: a firefighter party]

But then, just a few days later, he abruptly changed course: "I want a Darth Vader party!" Darth Vader? Where in heck did that come from? The kid had never even seen a Star Wars movie.

Cassie, who had already begun imagining the cute fire-engine-red decorations, was not pleased. "Darth Vader?" she said. "No, no...you said you wanted a..."

"Hey!" I interrupted. "You heard the kid. He says he wants a Darth Vader party. It's his birthday, after all."

You see, a long time ago, in a galaxy far, far away, I was sort of a Star Wars nut. It all started when I was a grossly underpaid, country radio station copywriter, in the midst of a quarter-life crisis. Right around that time, the first of the new Star Wars prequels was released, and it rekindled something inside that I hadn't felt since I was a kid. Once again I had a reason to live!

Suddenly I was spending the majority of the workday on eBay bidding for vintage toys , and it wasn't long before my apartment was transformed into a veritable Star Wars museum. Fortunately I already had a steady girlfriend.

In time I matured and grew out of my childish hobby – thank goodness – but I never fully got over the obsession. So when my son said he wanted a Darth Vader birthday, I was overcome with excitement.

For him, I mean.

Since neither of my kids had ever seen the movies, I felt it my fatherly duty to educate them on this staple of popular culture. So, the week before the birthday party, I made them...er...I mean, I let them watch the original Trilogy a couple times. It wasn't long before they were fully indoctrinated into George Lucas' magical world.

"Look, Daddy!" my son said while watching The Empire Strikes Back. "That's Yoga!"

"Hmmm, yeeess!" I responded. "Downward dog, I will do." Unfortunately the joke was completely lost on him.

"It's not Yo-GA," Boogieface corrected him. "It's Yo-DA!"

I was never so proud to be a father.

On the day of his birthday, I was...I mean...The Animal was giddy with anticipation. Cass dressed up Boogs like a little Princess Leia, and I even dug out my old Darth Vader costume from the basement, solely for my son's benefit, of course.

Then, right before the party, I gave both kids brand new plastic light sabers, which sent them running around the house like two little Jedi-in-training. I was beaming. (Note to parents: It might not be the best idea to give a large, sword-like weapon – plastic or not – to a rambunctious 3-year-old with little or no depth perception.)

The party itself was all that I dreamed it would be. For my son, I mean. We sang "Happy Birthday" to the tune of "The Imperial March," devoured a Star-Wars-themed cake, and then adjourned to the living room where The Animal tore into his pile of presents like a Rancor at an Ewok convention. (Google it.)

When it was all said and done, my boy had a treasure trove of new Star Wars toys. And just think, we were that close to having a bunch of boring firetrucks to play with.

For my son to play with, that is.

My Morning Madness

I fear the morning. Gone are those gentle, tranquil times when I'd get up, have some breakfast, and catch up on the morning headlines before heading off to work. Now it's zero to chaos in 4.2 seconds, thanks to my kids, who unlike me do not require caffeine to function at full capacity.

Here's an average morning at our house:

After showering and getting dressed, I go to wake up the kids so we can get them ready to go to preschool. The Animal shoots out of bed, smiling from ear to ear, ready to wreak havoc on the world. Boogieface just grunts and refuses to budge, despite several attempts to rouse her from her slumber. I leave her for my wife to deal with.

"Can I have some hot tea and play with your iPad, pleeeaaasssee!?" he says as I plop him on the couch. As I carry my son downstairs, he gives me his normal good-morning lick up the side of my face. How lovely.

"Sure, buddy. What do you want for breakfast?

"Uuumm? I want a blanna [translation: banana] with peanut butter and a waffle with syrup and cimamim [translation: cinnamon].

When I return to the living room with The Animal's tea, my wife enters the room carrying my crying daughter, piggy-back style.

"Her toe hurts," says Cass, rolling her eyes.

Boogs corrects her, sobbing: "It hurts SOOOOO bad! OWWWWWW!!" You'd think the toe must be broken or something, considering how hysterical she is. But as it turns out, it just hurts because she's getting too big for her footie pajamas, and her big toe is pushing too hard against the fabric. She has a similar reaction whenever she gets a splinter.

"Do you want us to take you to the hospital," Cassie asks, "because if you don't stop crying, that's what we're going to have to do."

My daughter's eyes widen. "NOOOOO!" she screams, tears streaming down her face as she clutches her toe. It's like we just told her we were going to have to amputate.

Right around this time my wife realizes we haven't bathed either of our kids for four, maybe five days. So as she drags them to the shower, a trail of grease and dirt in their wake, I escape to the kitchen to make lunches. There's a lot of yelling and screaming and crying coming from the bathroom, and for once I'm happy to be making peanut-butter cracker sandwiches.

Minutes later, Boogs emerges from the bathroom, still grumpy but fully dressed. Apparently we have holy water in our pipes because, miraculously, her big toe no longer hurts. However, now she's close to tears because her tights "feel weird." This is her normal response anytime we have her put on tights, socks, leggings, underwear, jeans, or shoes. And if you don't get them on quickly and correctly the first time—forget about it. She'll rip them off and throw them across the room, refusing to put them back on. She's our little angel.

When The Animal emerges from the bathroom, soaking wet and naked, he proceeds to run around the house screaming like a lunatic until Cass can hog-tie him and get him clothed.

After finishing their lunches, I give them their breakfast and beg them to eat it in under an hour. By the time I get them strapped into their car seats, I'm only 25 minutes late for work. A new record.

And that is what I get to wake up to every morning.

You know, looking back over this recap, it seems like my wife got the worst of it. On the other hand, I did have to make eight peanut-butter cracker sandwiches.

So that pretty much evens things out.

Just Another Day

Upon arriving home from work, I am enthusiastically greeted by my two loving offspring who are out in the backyard playing "Pirate", otherwise known as "Dig A Big Hole In The Middle Of The Yard And Throw Stuff In It."

I enter the house and greet my wife, who is busy preparing a lovely meal that the kids will never eat. I then navigate my way through the toy minefield that is my house to go and hang up my coat.

Just before dinner, The Animal and Boogieface come in from playing outside. My son's face is caked in mud and he has a mouthful of dirt because, according to his sister, he was eating a "dirty icicle." Boogs is holding a large, dirt-covered rock that she dug out of the yard. She gets a couple mixing bowls out of the cupboard, sits down in the middle of the kitchen floor, and proceeds to wash her new "pet", who she names Rocky IV, since she already has three other pet rocks up in her room, not to mention around 600 stuffed animals.

After we rinse most of the dirt from The Animal's mouth, the four of us sit down for what is sure to be yet another memorable family gathering. After saying grace and covering our ears to shield them from my son's deafening "AMEN!" scream, we spend the rest of the meal trying to get him to eat his cooked carrots, which to him, based on his reaction, taste like cooked cockroaches.

Following dinner, I flee to the living room with a book and a cup of coffee, as my wife continues to try to coerce the boy into eating. When she finally manages to get a carrot slice into his mouth, he gags and throws up all over himself, his food, the floor, and her. Dinner is officially over.

After we get The Animal cleaned and changed into his pajamas, Cass decides to run a couple errands (i.e., escape) around town. I am left to fend for myself. I return to the living room to drink my now cold cup of coffee and attempt to read just one page of my book without interruption.

Meanwhile my son uses the bathroom and goes No. 2 but doesn't tell anyone. Or wipe. He just puts his jammies back on and goes about his business. I find out about it later, after the damage has already been done.

After changing The Animal's underwear, I am summoned by Boogieface to the kitchen for a "party," complete with hors d'oeuvres (raisins, fruit squeezies, fruit strips) refreshments (milk, water), and music (the local pop radio station). As the three of us dance around the kitchen, hand-in-hand, to LMFAO's "I'm Sexy and I Know It," my mood gradually improves as the chaos that has been the last couple hours of my life melts away in the immeasurable love that I feel for my children.

That is, of course, until the chaos is reincarnated the following day, and the next day, and the next day…

My wife returns just in time for the nightly bedtime ritual. We each take a kid, hoping that by separating them we'll have a better chance of surviving the experience.

Finally, Cass and I have the house all to ourselves. I celebrate by abruptly falling asleep on the couch.

After all, tomorrow's another day. And I have to rest up.

The Great Indoors

Recently I went camping with Boogieface. It was freezing, the ground was hard, and the tent reeked of mold. I didn't sleep a wink.

Did I mention we were in her bedroom?

Ever since I've had kids I've been itching to take them camping. After all, there's nothing quite like being out in the woods and roughing it with nothing but a tent and a sleeping bag (and maybe a camping pillow, foam sleeping pad, lawn chair, iPad, iPod, Kindle, bottle of wine, some chicken parm, chocolate cake, and coffee). But since I wasn't sure how Boogs would handle sleeping in a tent for the first time, I decided to do a test run by setting up camp in her bedroom.

My friends and I used to go camping at least once a year as a way to keep in touch. Of course our last camp out kinda put an end to that.

It was several years ago now, but I'll never forget the date: January 4. Our lives were starting to get busier around that time, and it was the only day we could all agree on. Besides, we weren't novices. Cass and I had all the proper winter camping gear – wicking clothing, zero-degree sleeping bags, red wine, etc. – and, thanks to the Internet, we new how to keep warm out in the wild. We weren't worried.

At first.

As the day approached, however, the forecast wasn't looking good; the high temperature was supposed to be in the single digits. I kept waiting (hoping) for everyone to back out, but only one of my friends did, and of course we teased him mercilessly for it. There was no way we could back out now.

When we hit the trail head, the temperature was a balmy -4 degrees. One of my friends took a swig on his bottle and the water immediately crystallized on his beard. By the time that we reached our primitive camp site, an hour-and-a-half hike into the Allegheny National Forest, all the water we had brought along with us had frozen solid. The only liquid that didn't freeze was a case of beer that one of the guys had brought. We spent the day chopping firewood and guzzling cans of beer in the one minute we had before it too froze solid. At one point I looked over to see my wife standing so close to the fire that her pants where smoking and her new boots were melting. That night we slept in an improvised lean-to as close to the fire as we could get, hoping we wouldn't die in our sleep.

Good times!

Luckily, my first camping experience with Boogs wasn't as cold. But it was close. Hers is the coldest room in our 124-year-old, uninsulated home. You could hang meat in there. Usually I just sleep in my gutchies, but considering the situation, I decided to put on a pair of pajama pants and a sweatshirt. Figured I'd be fine.

Around 3 o'clock in the morning, I awoke, trembling from the cold despite my PJs and two fleece blankets. A couple times I thought about sneaking out and crawling into my nice warm bed in the other room, but I didn't want my daughter to think I wussed out. So I just borrowed one of her blankets.

My little angel, meanwhile, looked snug as a bug next to me, out cold in her Dora the Explorer fold-out bed. At one point I looked over and she didn't even have the covers on. I checked her pulse, just to make sure, but she was fine.

I gotta get me some of them footy pajamas.

The rest of the night I tossed and turned, trying unsuccessfully to find a comfortable position on the old hardwood floor. The only good thing was I didn't have to put on my boots to get out and take a pee. Plus, unlike my sub-zero camp out with my friends, there was little chance that I'd freeze to death.

Which gave me some comfort.

Just Another Day In Paradise

Sometimes when you're a parent, you just lose it. You can't help it. You're tired, you have a crappy day at work, and when you come home all you want is a little peace and quiet, but you get chaos.

And then you lose it.

It was partially my fault. That Sunday night I had tried to stretch out the weekend as long as possible. Of course at the time I didn't care. I knew I'd be dragging the next day. But, heck, that was tomorrow. And tomorrow was Monday. And Mondays are always, well, Mondays.

But then tomorrow came, as it usually does, and I just couldn't seem to get going. Then my back, which as usual had been fine all weekend, tightened into a knot again, and I spent most of the day wriggling around in my office chair. By the end of the workday, all I wanted to do was go home and take a nap.

But of course, parents of young children don't have that kind of freedom. So when I got home I immediately started grilling some steak and chicken as my wife and her sister took my two little ones and my niece for a walk around the block. It was actually a nice day to grill out, and for a moment I thought I'd be able to come out of my funk and salvage what was left of the day.

But then it was time for dinner.

A half an hour later everyone was finished eating. Except, of course, for my son. These days getting him to eat anything that isn't coated in chocolate or made of sugar is nearly impossible. As a result, every dinnertime turns into a marathon event as he whines about whatever is on his plate and refuses to let a vegetable anywhere in the vicinity of his mouth. Usually my wife takes it from here as I escape to the kitchen to clean up. Tonight, however, she and her sister had plans. Therefore, I was left to deal with The Animal on my own.

After cleaning off the table and loading the dishwasher, I headed to the living room where my niece and daughter were watching a cinematic classic: "Harry and the Hendersons." Meanwhile my son remained in his high chair, still complaining about the chicken and peas still left on his plate.

"Daaaaddy!" he called out from the dining room. "Do I have to eat my peas too or just my chicken?"

"All of it!" I snapped back. Sometimes I give in, just to put an end to the whining. But today I was in no mood to negotiate. "Your peas AND your chicken! And I don't want to hear another word until you're done!"

"But Daaaaddy…"

"NOT ANOTHER WORD!!"

I knew it was silly to get so worked up. But I couldn't help it. When you go through the same scenario every single day, it gets a little old.

I reclined in my chair and tried to escape in the movie. My niece, however, who is incapable of staying put for more than two seconds, was bouncing around the living room like Tigger and asking me question after question.

"Uncle Val," she said. "Is that hairy guy a Bigfeet?"

"Yes," I replied. "And he's a BigFOOT, not a BigFEET."

"Uncle Val…does the Bigfeet, I mean, BigFOOT, really live with them in their house?"

"Yes."

"Uncle Val…is the Bigfeet's name Harry?"

"Please just watch the movie," I said, closing my eyes in the hopes of ending the inquisition.

Just then The Animal cried out again from the dining room. "Daaaaddy! Do I have to eat all my peas too or just my chicken?"

"YES!" I barked, my patience at an end. "And you only have five more minutes to finish your dinner or you're going straight to bed. YOU UNDERSTAND ME?!?!"

"But Daaaaddy…"

"FIVE MORE MINUTES!!!"

Moments later I was hovering over my son, his Lightning McQueen fork in my hand, shoveling the chicken and peas into his mouth. I had lost it. And I knew it. I could hear myself talking just like one of those grouchy old fathers I'd see when I was a kid, the ones who were always yelling and miserable. The ones I swore I'd never be like when I was a dad. But I just couldn't take it anymore. "And you can forget about the movie," I said. "You're going straight to bed after this!"

That did it. Now the tears began streaming down his little ketchup-covered face.

I felt terrible. He's going to remember this, I thought. From now on he's going to think I'm a mean daddy. He'll probably be talking about this very moment years from now while sitting in therapy. I felt so guilty. I felt guilty for yelling at a three-year-old and getting all bent out of shape over some lousy peas and chicken. For ignoring my niece's questions. For being unable to control my temper. But I couldn't help it. I just wanted things to be easy again.

Then, right in the middle of it all, as he sat there sniffling and chewing his food, my son smiled ever-so-slightly, looked up at me and whispered, "You're the best daddy in the world."

It was like a punch to the stomach. Suddenly all my anger and frustration melted away, and I felt a heaviness lifted from my shoulders. Someone Up There knew just what I needed.

With tears now welling up in my own eyes, I bent down and kissed him. "And you know what?" I said. "You're the best son in the world. Go ahead. You can go watch the movie now."

As my little guy jumped out of his chair and ran off to the living room to join his sister and cousin, I heard him say to them, "Guess what? I MADE DADDY HAPPY!"

And for the first time that day, I was.

OK, Daddy—Let Go!

I was doing some overdue spring yard work when my daughter called me from my wife's phone.

"Daddy," she said, "can you bring me my big bike? I wanna show them how I can do it!"

It was the first really warm spring day of the year, and all of the neighborhood kids were riding their bikes at the park around the corner, trying to shake off the rust of a long, cold winter.

We had spent most of the day wandering around The Beav soaking up some much needed Vitamin D. Cass and I walked while Boogieface and The Animal zipped around us on their balance bikes.

If you're not familiar, a balance bike is just a normal bike, sans pedals. To make it move you just put your feet on the ground and push until you have some momentum. Then you lift up your feet and see how far you can glide.

It's the kind of bike Pebbles or Bam-Bam would have had, minus the granite tires.

My daughter actually has a real bike (i.e., her "big bike") with actual pedals and training wheels, but she's never been too confident on it. So after we saw how quickly my son got used to his balance bike, we decided to get one for Boogs as well.

As Cass and I walked around town that day, basking in the rare Western PA sunshine, the kids rode ahead on their pedal-free two-wheelers. At one point The Animal stopped too abruptly and ended up flipping over his handlebars to the sidewalk below. Luckily his face broke his fall. Boogs, on the other hand, was really surprising us with her skill and confidence, fearlessly cruising down hills she would have been terrified of just last fall.

Later on when we got home, she surprised me again when she said she wanted me to take the training wheels off of her "big bike" to see if she could ride it. Considering she usually gets off of her bike to push it over cracks in the sidewalk, I wasn't getting my hopes up.

But as I ran alongside her holding the handlebars, I could tell she was really close to figuring it out. With each pass up the driveway, she became more confident (and my lower back became more stiff). After a while we decided to call it quits for the day and continue with the training another time.

So I was a little surprised when she called me from the park later that afternoon. I still didn't think she was ready to fly solo. But I figured at least the park had a nice soft surface to cushion her fall.

Boogs saw me coming down the alley with her bike and darted across the park to meet me. Hopping on her purple Trek, she asked me to help her get going.

And then she said it: "OK, Daddy—let go!"

So I did. And suddenly, in the blink of an eye, my little girl wasn't so little anymore. I ran alongside her, unable to register what I was seeing. I felt like I was in one of those financial planning commercials you always see on TV. ("She's growing up so fast. Are you doing what it takes to make sure you're ready for her future?")

Later on that night we were getting the kids ready for bed when we were again surprised, this time by The Animal who, inspired by his sister's momentous day, decided he was ready to take a big step too. "I'm gonna pee like a big guy!" he said, dropping his footie pajamas to the floor and taking a stance in front of the toilet. I darted over to help, but before I could get there he gave the wall a good soaking.

I guess he's not ready to fly solo just yet. But that too will come in time.

10 Things That Can Make My 5-Year-Old Freak Out

The following is a list of things that can send Boogieface into an inconsolable crying hissy fit. There are countless others, of course, but these are the top 10:

10 THINGS THAT CAN MAKE MY 5-YEAR-OLD FREAK OUT

10) Her sock doesn't "feel right."

9) Her tights "feel weird."

8) She gets a splinter.

7) Her brother hugs her too hard.

6) Her brother licks her.

5) Reorganizing the mountain of dolls and stuffed animals on her bed without her expressed written consent.

4) Any deviation from the norm.

3) Her dippy egg is too dippy.

2) Her dippy egg isn't dippy enough.

1) No particular reason whatsoever.

The Bloody Giraffe

"Look, Daddy!" says my daughter, holding out a picture of a rainbow-colored giraffe. "I did it!"

I was picking the kids up from day care and, as always, Boogieface couldn't wait to show me her Crayola masterpiece of the day.

"It's beautiful, honey! Look how well you stayed in between the lines!"

Then The Animal turns the corner with his...well...work of art. "Look, Dadda!" he says, holding up the same picture of a giraffe. But unlike my daughter's multi-colored interpretation, his is just one big red scribble.

"Ooooh," I say, crouching down to his level, "a red giraffe! That's really cool!"

Just then he comes close, like he's going to tell me a secret, and whispers in my ear: "It's not red...IT'S BLOOD!"

Yikes.

I admit it: my son scares me. Sure, he may be just 3 years old, but the boy's a wild one.

You're never really safe when you're in the same room with The Animal. Take your eyes off him for one moment and suddenly he's launching himself from atop the sofa and onto your head, where he digs in with his claws and holds on like a leopard subduing its prey. At any moment your face could be the target of a flying Matchbox car or a hard-plastic Stegosaurus. The other day he took me down with a blast to the shin with my old Gaiking Shogun Warrior. Your only defense is to constantly keep him in your sights.

Either that or dress in full hockey goalie gear.

Woody plays dead. It's his only defense.

So when he tells me that his picture is a blood-soaked giraffe, I'm obviously concerned. Suddenly I'm having visions of future: expulsions from school, juvenile detention hearings, monthly visits through a prison security window.

Later on I share the disturbing story with my wife, who approaches The Animal, cautiously of course, and asks him why his giraffe is bloody? I'm fully expecting him to say something like, "Because I deaded him!" or "Because the voices told me to do it."

But then all my fears are abated.

"Because he had a bloody nose!" he says. That's when we remember that earlier that morning he had woken up with a bloody nose and it had gotten all over himself and his bed. Hence the bloody giraffe.

Whew! What a relief. Turns out my son is not some deranged psychopath after all. Wildly unpredictable and dangerous to be around—sure. But a psychopath? Nah.

Stupid Plastic Elmo

"Dadda, can I give this to the baby for him to keep?" We were at at Café Kolache. The Animal, his face smeared with chocolate from his usual Saturday morning "Fluffy" (hot chocolate topped with whipped cream) was holding his tiny plastic toy Elmo.

"Uh…sure, buddy," I said. "I mean, if you really want to." I was stunned. After all, this wasn't just any old toy. This was Elmo. Now he wanted to give it away to some random 18-month-old at the next table.

"Here you go…you can keep it!" said my son, handing over his once beloved Elmo to the smiling baby, who immediately thrust the forsaken toy into his slobbery mouth.

Then, as he sat back down at our table, The Animal took a bite from his kolache and said, "Dat was a BABY toy, and I don't want to play with baby toys anymore."

It was at that moment that I realized this was the last time I'd ever see that Elmo toy again. I felt like someone had just punched me in the stomach.

But why? I never understood why he liked that stupid toy anyway. You couldn't pose it or move its arms or legs around. It just stood there like a statue. I don't even remember the last time he even watched Elmo, which used to be his favorite part of Sesame Street. The same thing had happened with Boogieface when she was around the same age.

One day Elmo is the center of the universe, the next he's The Planet Formerly Known as Pluto.

Personally, I couldn't care less if we ever heard Elmo's squeaky, high-pitched, baby-talking voice again. But when my son gave Stupid

Plastic Elmo away, it signified something greater—that my kids are growing up right before my eyes, and I am helpless to stop it.

It's too bad. Stupid Plastic Elmo probably would've made The Animal's Toy Hall of Fame (a plastic bin in the basement) along with his other favorite toys, like his wooden spoon-handle pig, bear, and cow; his "Hooker" (a string with a hook on it from one of his Playmobil® toys), his "Stringer" (an old shoestring), and a dozen or so other once-cherished toys that I just can't bear to get rid of.

I'm pretty sure this is how hoarders are born. One minute you're saving your kid's favorite old toys, the next you're sharing your dumpster-like home with 37 cats.

And it's not just the toys that I have a hard time parting with. It's my daughter's favorite old pink cowgirl boots or my son's old monster tossle cap. It pains me to have to take them down to the basement and cast them into the yard sale pile, where, like inmates on death row, they await their official and permanent exit from our lives.

These things aren't just random toys and objects. They're Saturday mornings at the café and lazy afternoons on the front porch. They're talismans that helped us survive hour-long church services and seemingly endless waits at the restaurant. Stupid Plastic Elmo – boring as he was – represented some of the most cherished times I've spent with my children. Now he was leaving our lives forever, unceremoniously I might add, lodged snugly between the gums of someone else's kid.

Ah, but such is life. I can't stop my kids from getting older anymore than I can stop the hair from growing on my ears. (I think I may be turning into a Sasquatch.)

So, farewell to thee, Stupid Plastic Elmo. Thanks for everything you did to keep The Animal distracted whilst he waited for his "pisketti and meatballs," or when Mommy was stuck in line at the grocery store, or when Father's sermon went just a little too long. Hopefully you can do the same for the family of the kid who jammed you into his slimy, germ-riddled mouth at our last parting.

Don't forget us. We'll certainly never forget you.

And So It Begins—The School Years

Wait... that's it? No tears? No screaming "Daddy! No! Don't leave me!", while she clutches onto my leg in desperation?

Already having funIt was my daughter's first day of kindergarten at Sts. Peter and Paul Catholic School, my old stomping grounds, where I'd spent eight long years learning, making friends, and occasionally tormenting the nuns. (I even wrote a book about it. Luckily my daughter can't read just yet.)

But when it came time for Mommy and Daddy to skedaddle, I could barely get my daughter to acknowledge me as I asked her for a kiss goodbye. She was too busy playing My Little Ponies with her new "friends," if you could even call them that. I mean, com'on, she just met them 5, maybe 10 minutes earlier. I've been around since the beginning, almost six years of steadfast dedication, and the most I get is a half-hearted peck on my way out?

So much for gratitude.

I'd been dreading this day for some time now. The day when we'd be sending our little baby off to begin the next phase in her life: The School Years. This is big. Now that she's off in the real world, we won't be able to shield her from outside influences. Pretty soon she'll find out about things like PS2s, Miley Cyrus (heaven help us), and white bread. (The girl didn't even know what an Oreo was up until a few days ago.) Sure, she'll be making new friends that will last a lifetime, but she'll also be experiencing peer pressure and bullying and all the other rotten things kids do to each other as practice for adulthood.

And I haven't even mentioned homework.

I don't remember all that much about my own kindergarten experience except that it took place in this little, wooden, one-room school house a few miles up the road. You'd think I lived in Walnut Grove or something. (Google it.) My teacher was Mrs. Harris, a wonderful woman who set the bar for every other instructor throughout my academic career. It was there where I first met friends I'd spend much of the next 12 years of my life with, first at S.S.P.P. and then in high school. It was also there where I chewed through the sleeves of my Steelers pleather jacket – kindergarten stress, I suppose – and then blamed it on my friend J.C. I don't think Mom bought it, though.

When kids reach school age, it doesn't just change their life, it changes that of the parents as well. Suddenly there's Christmas pageants and science fairs and parent-teacher conferences and dozens of other new things to further complicate your already busy calendar. And let's not forget about the germs your kid will pick up from their classmates and then bring home to pass along to you. Wonderful. I'm banking my PTO days now in anticipation of being sick from October until the end of April.

The hardest part for me though about sending my daughter off to school is knowing that I won't be experiencing it with her. This is her first step in becoming an independent person. She'll be making her own memories now, very few of which will involve yours truly. And I don't like it. Not one bit. That's one of the things I love about being a dad: having at least two people on this planet (possibly three) who actually need me from time to time. My daughter actually still admires me and thinks I'm pretty smart. Go figure. With most of the girls throughout my life, including my wife, this feeling of appreciation wore off pretty quickly. We're talking months. But not with my baby girl. She still thinks Daddy is a pretty cool dude, and I'd like to keep it that way as long as possible.

She's my last hope.

Part of me feels a little jealous. After all, she's starting what will be the best years of her life, forging friendships that will last a lifetime. Another part of me, however, feels kind of sorry for her. I mean, once you start going to school, it's over. No more doing whatever you want during the weekdays. No more sleeping in from September through May. For the next 17 years or so she'll only have three months of carefree living each year. After that she'll just be another poor working schlep like the rest of us.

It was pretty tough leaving my daughter in that classroom that first morning. My wife shed a few tears when we left the building, and I admit I fought off a few myself. I know I have to learn to let go, to let her continue to grow and learn. It's just that, up until this point, she was all ours. Our little girl. Now she's about to become someone else for so many other people. And I'm not sure I'm ready to share just yet.

Ah, but what can I do? Such is life. I can't keep my little girl from growing up anymore than I can keep these freakishly long white hairs from growing out of my forehead from time to time. (What's that all about anyway?)

At least I can take comfort that she's going to my old alma mater, where I know she'll be in good hands. I just hope she doesn't find out about my book. Then I may have some explaining to do.

The Animal vs. The Apple

The way he was carrying on you'd think we'd told my son they'd cancelled Christmas. We just wanted him to try an apple, for Pete's sake.

"This is the new rule:" said my wife, in her official Mommy-has-had-enough voice. "From now on, if you want to eat sweets, you're gonna have to start eating fruits and vegetables with every meal." It was a shocking declaration, considering my son would sooner eat a cockroach than a cucumber, let alone any type of fruit. But if Mommy doth declare it, you might as well chisel it in stone. It's the law.

From day one The Animal has loved bananas, or as he calls them, "blannas." But as far as fruit goes, that's it. No berries. No grapes. Heck, we can't even get the boy to try watermelon – the candy of fruit! He's 3 ½ years old and he's never even tasted an apple. Applesauce, sure. But nary a Granny Smith, a McIntosh, or a Red Delicious. It's not like we haven't tried. But feeding him fruit is like trying to give medicine to a Labrador—it's just not happening.

But tonight we were going up street for ice cream, and we decided that if he wanted to partake, he'd have to at least try an apple. And, boy, he wasn't happy about it.

"Dadda?" he said through a flood of tears. "Can I just have a little bitty crumb of an apple and then I can have ice cream?"

"We'll see, buddy. Just try it and then we'll talk about it." I was sure that if we could just get him to try the darn apple, he'd love it. I mean, com'on, it's an apple. Even Eve couldn't resist.

After a while it was getting late and we were running out of time to go up street. "Fine," I said, "you don't have to try it. But we're leaving now and you're not getting any ice cream, understand?"

Turn up the tear machine. "No, Dadda! I want ice cream!!!"

Part of me really wanted to cave, to let the boy off the hook. But then again this was crazy. All we were asking was that he try a ridiculously small piece of an apple. So for once I stood firm.

Faced with the threat of an ice-creamless evening, The Animal blinked first. "OK, Dadda, I'll try it – but nobody look at me!" That's his thing. Whenever he agrees to try a new type of food, no one's allowed to watch. Not me, not Momma, not even his big sis. It's like he doesn't want us to take any enjoyment from our victory.

But saying he'll do it and actually doing it are two different things. For the next fifteen minutes or so, he walked around the house, whimpering and crying while carrying a miniscule, half-of-a-half-of-a-pea-sized piece of gala apple on his spoon, every so often pleading with his mother and I to spare him this torturous task. But we were sticking to our guns.

Finally, he went into the other room, closed both doors behind him, and…well, he still wouldn't try it.

I'd reached the end of my patience. "OK, that's it—no ice cream. Com'on, we're leaving."

"NO, DADDA!" he wailed, clutching onto my leg and hyperventilating in the cutest, most pathetic way.

It was time to put an end to this nonsense right here and now. "All right, this is your last chance! Open your mouth…" I took the spoon and put it up to his lips and, after one final whimper, he finally ate the apple. Hallelujah!

"Way to go, buddy!" I said, trying my best to make a big deal out of it. "I knew you could do it. Now wasn't that yummy?"

"Yeah," he admitted between sniffles.

"Great!" I said, thinking we'd finally made a breakthrough. "You want some more?"

"No. Can we go get ice cream now, Dadda?"

And so, yet another dinnertime battle had come to a close with no clear victor. Although, we went up street and got ice cream, so I guess we all won in the end.

Morning Meltdowns

It was the perfect morning. A pre-dawn run. Cartoons with my son. An egg, avocado, cheddar, capicola, and Tabasco (Chipotle style) breakfast sandwich. It was all going so well.

Until…

Boogieface was wearing her cute little plaid uniform and, for the first time this year, a pair of red knee socks. The socks were thicker than her normal white ones, but it was a chilly morning so they seemed appropriate.

We were on schedule, amazingly, so I told her to put on her shoes so we could head off to school before I went to work. But as soon as she put them on I knew a meltdown was coming. After five-plus years, I can just sense these things.

"These socks don't feel good," she said.

Uh, oh.

I tried to rush her out of the house before things had a chance to escalate. "They're fine," I said. "You're just not used to them. Trust me, you won't even notice them by the time you get to school."

Yeah, right.

"No, Daddy. They just don't feel good." By now the tears were welling up in her eyes and her voice was starting to squeak. WARNING: Meltdown imminent!

When my daughter puts something on and says it "doesn't feel good," you can pretty much kiss it goodbye, because she's about to rip it off and throw it across the room. And you're never getting her to try it on again. Ever. She's a nut-job. Cute as a button, but a nut-job nonetheless.

I pushed her into the car. "Look, just get in your car seat and buckle up, honey. We're gonna be late."

But by now the tears were flowing. "No! No! I'm not wearing them!"

I could feel my blood beginning to boil. Stay calm, Val. Don't blow up. We've been here before, and you know she doesn't respond well to yelling. Just take a deep breath and reason with her. "Look, Boogs… we're going to be late. You're just going to have to…"

"I WANT DIFFERENT SOCKS!"

So much for diplomacy. "Son of a b____!" I slammed the car door and headed back towards the house. So much for staying calm. "Cassie!" I yelled. "It's useless. She won't…"

But before I could finish, my wife was already at the door holding another pair of shoes. "These are one size bigger," she said. "See if they make her socks feel any better."

I stomped back to the car and opened the door. "Here. Try these. They're bigger and have more room and…"

But she wasn't going for it. "No. I am not wearing those shoes!" Then she pulled her legs in and ripped off her shoes and socks, dropping them to the floor.

Now I was at Def-Con 4. Once again I slammed the door and went back inside to fetch a different, less bulky pair of socks. "She's insane!" I said as I brushed past my wife. Then I went back out to the car with the new socks, fuming and flustered and muttering to myself just like all those crazy parents I said I'd never be like.

A few minutes later I was still irritated as I dropped her off at school. But looking into her still teary eyes and seeing her there in her pigtails and oversized pink-leopard-print backpack, it was difficult to stay mad. So I kissed her goodbye, told her I loved her, and went back to my car to head off to work. Meanwhile I could sense a whole new batch of gray hairs sprouting from my head.

Heaven help us when she's a teenager.

Morning Mayhem

The morning is by far my favorite time of day. For a while, at least. Like an hour. At most. After that it just all goes to crap.

It always starts out just fine...

After my alarm goes off or The Animal wakes me – both unsettling ways to begin the day – and we head downstairs where I make him his hot tea with honey while he takes in a cartoon. I then go off to shave, shower, and get ready for work.

By the time I'm dressed, my wife is awake and she makes sure Boogieface is up and getting ready for school. At this point we're just about a half an hour into the day.

So far, so good.

Next we make breakfast for the kiddos, and I implore them to please eat quickly so that we can leave on time for once. This is right around the 45-minute mark, and it's at this point when things begin to break down. After all, my kids still have to brush their hair, brush their teeth, go "pee-pee on the potty," and get their shoes and coats on—a veritable minefield of tasks, any one of which can end up in disaster.

My son, surprisingly, is the more manageable one at this early hour. After woofing down his bowl of peanut butter and banana and guzzling his third sippy cup of hot tea (he may have a drinking problem), he hurries off to finish getting ready, just so he'll have a few minutes to play before we leave.

At least he has his priorities straight.

Things aren't as simple with my daughter. If we're fortunate enough to get her dressed and downstairs without a meltdown – by no means a simple task – from that point on she moves at a turtle's pace, savoring each bite of her waffle like it's her final meal. When she finally finishes her breakfast, she moves, sloth-like, toward the bathroom to brush her hair. But of course she can never locate the brush, even though it's always in the same drawer. Eventually she begins to brush her hair. Slowly. Her eyes glazed over like she's still off in dreamland.

"Com'on…let's go!," says my wife for the hundredth time in the past five minutes. "Daddy's going to be late!"

But, alas, by now we're already late, and we've yet to have our daily argument with my daughter about what coat she's going to wear, and that, yes, she has to wear one, and that she's old enough now to be tying her own shoes, for goodness sake. If we're lucky, she won't have a "My sock feels weird!" moment or suddenly remember that it's Bake-A-Batch-of-Muffins-for-the-Entire-Class-Day at school (both common occurrences). Otherwise we could be here for hours.

The calm of the morning is now a distant memory and has given way to a hectic, anxiety-filled time of yelling and rushing and general frustration over the fact that we go through this same ridiculous ritual every single morning, and that I'm going to be late for work, again, and that tomorrow we're just going to have to get up earlier, which will never happen, of course, because we're always so tired from the dreaded Bedtime Ritual, which is mentally and physically draining, and which usually leads me to have one glass of wine too many.

Luckily we get to wake up and do it all over again tomorrow.

Five Signs There's Trouble A-Brewin'

5) When my son says, "What's that green stuff?", pointing to the chopped up veggies my wife tried to conceal within the meatloaf.

4) When it's way past their bedtime and they say, "But I'm not tired!"

3) When my son wants cereal, and I try to pass off almond milk for 2% milk, because we're all out of 2% milk, and he says, "This milk tastes funny…"

2) When one of them says, "Hey…where's my drawing?", just after I've tossed said drawing in the garbage and topped it with old coffee grinds.

1) When my daughter says, "My sock doesn't feel good…", just as we're trying to get out the door.

Elf on the Shelf—Like I Don't Have Enough to Do Already

I jump out of bed, my heart racing. Stopping in the doorway, I poke my head out into the hallway and listen closely for any signs of life. Then, stealthily, I move out onto the landing, careful to avoid the squeaky floorboards that could betray my position.

As I begin to tip-toe down the stairs, I hear something. Movement. Again I halt and hold my breath in the early morning darkness, listening closely before continuing my descent.

Then, just before reaching the bottom, I hear a thud. Footsteps. And then a door opening.

The Animal has awakened!!

With no time to lose, I sprint into the den where I find Snowflake – our Elf on the Shelf – still in his previous day's perch above the window. Grabbing him, I make a b-line to the living room and toss him into the Christmas tree, making sure he's securely in place on one of the higher branches.

Mission accomplished. And just in time, too.

We got suckered into this whole Elf-on-the-Shelf thing last year after my sister-in-law purchased one for the kids, unbeknownst to my wife and me. After being unwillingly thrust into it, we had no choice but to go along with the ruse.

Honestly, I don't mind that much. It's actually pretty cute to see my kids' little faces light up as they come downstairs in the morning to discover that Snowflake is no longer where they saw him last. They then head off in different directions, searching the first floor for any signs of Santa's little spy.

Suddenly, one of them cries out, "Daddy! Come look! I found Snowflake!"

Still not completely awake, I put on my best poker face and feign surprise. "Wow!" I say. "How'd he get way up there?" Knowing full well, of course, how he got way up there. Daddy put him there. At 4:30 this morning, when he got up to take a pee and suddenly remembered.

The problem is I can't move the stupid thing to its new location each night until after the kids have gone to bed and we're certain they're asleep. Boogieface has never come downstairs on her own after going to bed, so we never have to worry about her. The Animal, on the other hand, will stay quiet for an hour or so before suddenly appearing in the living room with his blankie in hand, thumb firmly planted in his mouth.

This could lead to disaster if at that particular moment yours truly is in the act of moving Snowflake to his new location.

So I usually wait until late at night before doing anything. Problem is, by that time I've had a couple glasses of Cabernet and I tend to forget about the elf when I go up to bed. Because of this, I've had to come downstairs several times now in the early morning just to move it.

And during that early hour, when I'm tip-toeing around the house like a cat burglar, climbing the furniture to place that little felt-covered and footless (What's up with that, by the way?) doll somewhere out of my kids' reach, I can't help but think to myself, What has my life come to?

Alas, there's no way out of it now. We're stuck in this annual Christmastime charade until the kids stop believing. And come to think of it, I'm OK with that. After all, they won't be this innocent forever.

If only that stupid elf could move himself every night. That would be a Christmas miracle.

Oh, Christmas Tree

God bless my wife. All she wants is the perfect Christmas-Tree Decorating Day. You know, the one they always show on TV, where the fireplace is lit, the presents are wrapped, and everyone is singing Christmas carols around the tree. Meanwhile, through the window you can see the gently falling snowflakes coating the world in a blanket of white.

What a load of crap.

This year's holiday festivities began the day after Thanksgiving with our second annual tree-cutting outing. It was a sunny, blue-sky morning at the tree farm, which, thanks to a fresh snowfall, resembled a winter wonderland. Some good friends and their kids joined us for the day, too, saving us from having to be alone with each other, which rarely turns out good.

The kids were full of energy as they explored the acres of pines and romped around in the snow. Afterward we stopped for lunch at the cozy Log Cabin Inn, where I had my annual Sasquatch Burger. And surprisingly, despite the proximity to nap time, both The Animal and Boogieface were well-behaved. It was a mini Christmas miracle.

The tree-decorating phase? Not so good.

After I somehow managed to squeeze our Griswold-esque Fraser fir through the front door and into the living room, it was time for the adorning. Cassie, overflowing with Christmas spirit, turned on the holiday tunes and hauled the boxes of ornaments and decorations out of the basement. Boogieface beamed in anticipation, while The Animal, clearly overstimulated by the situation, screamed and yelled and bounced around the room like...well...a wild animal, which is pretty much what he's like every other day of the year. Meanwhile, I sat in the chair in the corner sipping on my coffee and hoping no one would notice me.

Don't get me wrong. It's not that I don't enjoy a beautifully decorated tree. I'd just prefer that someone else handle the actual decorating of it. Plus, I was trying not to panic about the growing mess of cardboard boxes, storage containers, tissue paper, glitter, ornaments, ornament hooks, candles, nutcrackers, strings of lights, nativity scenes, wreaths, garland, and all other manner of Christmas accouterments that had taken over the dining and living rooms. I just can't relax when things are a mess. I get all grumpy and stressed out thinking about all the work I'm going to have when we're done.

Makes me a real joy to be around. Just ask my wife.

But this year I really wanted to be in a good mood for Cassie. Or at the very least pretend. So I put down my coffee, pulled an ornament out of the box, and did my best to grin and bear it. Even though I knew what was coming.

Of course, it didn't take long for The Animal to locate the most breakable of ornaments and place it on the tree, where it stayed for about two seconds before losing its precarious hold on the branch and crashing to the wooden train platform below. Moments later Boogieface discovered her brother's favorite fire truck ornament and insisted that she be the one to place it on the tree. The Animal wasn't about to let this happen, of course, and he wailed and cried as he tried to wrest it from her grasp. We tried to reason with my daughter – HA! – telling her why giving the ornament to her brother was the right thing to do. But she was unmoved, sighting the immutable finders-keepers rule.

Now, as parents it's our job to take advantage of situations like this to teach our children and encourage them to always do what's right. So, when Boogs was distracted, Cassie quickly snatched the fire truck from her hands and gave it to The Animal. This, in turn, sent my first-born into a crying tantrum of her own.

Thus began the inevitable screaming-and-crying phase of Christmas-Tree Decorating Day.

By this point Cass was visibly frustrated, and I was wondering if it was too early for a glass of bourbon. As the crying and yelling continued, I quietly slipped away and started to clean up instead.

That was it. The joy of Christmas-Tree Decorating Day had lasted for a whopping seven minutes. Boogieface kept on crying and whining until we were compelled to send her to her room. Meanwhile The Animal continued his rampage, stomping fragile Christmas heirlooms into oblivion and trashing my train set like a mini Godzilla.

Like they say, it's the most wonderful time of the year.

An Evening With Friends
Ain't What it Used to Be

Last weekend, some friends invited us over for drinks and dinner. And in the dead of winter, especially an Antarctic winter like this one, getting out of the house for a little socializing with other adult human beings sounded heavenly. So I was really looking forward to it.

Until I found out that kids were invited too.

You see, our friends have three little girls and therefore invited us to bring along our offspring as well. There was also another couple and mother there too, and they added three more children to the mix. For those of you keeping score at home, that's eight kids and seven adults. We were outnumbered, which is never a good thing.

I remember back before we had kids when we'd gather with friends at a bar or maybe at someone's apartment, and there'd be music and food and drinks (and more drinks) and plenty of uncensored conversation about anything but diapers and breast pumps and proper time-out technique. It was wonderful.

Of course back then there were no 4-year-olds running through the room pushing an unnecessarily loud plastic toy lawnmower across the hardwood floor. There were no screams and yells and thuds coming from the other room that sent you running off to investigate and either administer First Aid or deliver a thorough tongue-lashing. There was no limiting yourself to just one or two glasses of wine because you still had to go home and make it through the dreaded bedtime ritual.

No, back then there was nothing but the pure joy of being with friends and a seemingly unlimited supply of Yuengling and Cabernet, or, depending on your politics, Budweiser and Mad Dog 20/20.

Times certainly have changed. Now when we hang out with friends, more often then not we have to bring the kids along, which pretty much guarantees a less than satisfying experience.

At first things weren't so bad. Upon arrival, our kids threw off their coats and took off to explore and, in my son's case, wreak havoc upon this strange new planet. Meanwhile I took a seat around the kitchen peninsula and settled in with a tasty micro brew, hoping my kids would disappear for at least an hour or two, whilst I munched on appetizers and caught up with friends.

Wishful thinking.

Over the next hour or so, as the adults hovered around the kitchen near the food and alcoholic beverages, the little lunatics (aka, our children), darted from room to room, screaming, yelling, whining, laughing, and fighting. It was hard to ignore, not that I didn't do my best to try. And of course, after a few glorious minutes of talking about anything but our children, eventually we slipped back into Parent Mode and started comparing notes on nap time techniques and potty training.

The worst part of the day, as with most days, came when it was time to feed the children, which meant that we had to interrupt their out-of-controlness and try to get them to sit still for a few seconds and eat something they had absolutely no interest in eating. This was my wife's idea. I was completely happy with just letting them continue whatever it was they were doing, as long as they were doing it somewhere far from me, so that I could continue to pretend it was 2006, or any other year before we had children. Unfortunately women have that darn nurturing instinct that compels them to feed their young.

In the end – and by that I mean 7:00 p.m. – it turned out to be a pretty enjoyable visit, thanks to the hospitality of our most generous hosts. And I have to admit it, the kids were pretty well-behaved for the most part (i.e., they mainly left us alone).

Afterward I had to wait out in the car with the kids for a half hour while my wife was still inside saying goodbye to everyone. But that's another story for another day.

My Phantom Fears

It was always there in the back of my mind. I knew I'd have to talk to them about it some day, but I wanted to hold off as long as possible. The thing is, it was inevitable they'd find out eventually, either from someone at school or from watching TV. I just wanted to shield them from it as long as I could.

But finally I decided it was time to show my kids "Star Wars: Episode I – The Phantom Menace."

My biggest concern, of course: Jar-Jar Binks. Ugh. I mean, what if they actually liked him? I don't know if I could go on after that.

Would they ever want to watch the original three movies again, which they love, even though they don't have all that fancy CGI crap that George Lucas has become so enamored with for some reason?

Or, like every other true Star Wars fan, would they be bored to death by the sub-par writing, hideous acting, and totally soulless and unlikable characters?

One could only hope.

The thing is, Episode I is like a gateway drug to the even more horrific Episodes II and III. I could be opening up can of worms of intergalactic proportions.

On the other hand, why was I so afraid? I mean, what's the worst that could happen? Who cares if my kids laughed at Jar-Jar's hijinks or if liked the three prequels better than the original films? They don't have to like everything their dad likes, right?

What am I saying!? Of course they do.

I guess it's not all that bad. Darth Maul is pretty sweet, with that wicked face paint, horns, and that super-cool double-ended light saber. The pod-racing scene is pretty darn awesome, too. And just because it annoys me to no end that Mr. Lucas decided to cast a bunch of big-name Hollywood actors instead of giving some fresh faces a chance to shine, a la Harrison Ford, Carrie Fisher, and Mark Hamill, doesn't mean that my kids will care. I mean, they don't know Samuel L. Jackson from Samuel Clemens.

Yet.

But in the end it all comes back to Jar-Jar. He's just unforgivable in my book. Even worse than those ridiculous Ewoks. Heck, C-3PO even seems cool next to him.

Jar-Jar notwithstanding, I decided to face my fears and let my kids watch it. And you know what? It wasn't as bad as I thought it would be. Their reaction, that is; the movie is still awful as all get out. And surprisingly, my kids barely even mentioned Mr. Binks. They were too busy trying to follow along with the film's ridiculously complicated and boring political plot line, which after about 10 minutes had my son fidgeting around and whining to watch something else.

His exact words: "I don't like this movie!"

That's my boy.

Funny, but he was never bored watching any of the original three Star Wars films, with their rudimentary special effects and then unknown actors. Interesting.

So it turns out that my fears were much ado about nothing. My kids aren't clamoring for me to buy them a Jar-Jar Binks action figure. And since both of them seemed bored out of their skulls by the movie, I doubt I'll ever have to sit through it again, thank goodness.

Next up: the Indiana Jones movies. At least the first three, that is. I'll deal with "The Kingdom of the Crystal Skull" when the time comes.

Top Five Myths About Parenthood

Parents are always giving out advice about parenthood, what it's like, how it changes your outlook, how it drains your zest for life and turns your hair gray and makes you consider faking your own death and escaping to some exotic island where no one will ever find you again.

And, for the most part, they're right.

But there are a few common myths about parenthood that I'd like to debunk once and for all.

So without further ado…

MY TOP 5 MYTHS ABOUT PARENTHOOD

Myth #5: Enjoy your kids. It all goes by so quickly.
Yeah, right. Let me tell you, I've been a parent for a little over six years now, and it's been the longest six years of my life. Heck, it seems more like 60. Which is appropriate, since that's also how old I feel.

Myth #4: Beware of The Terrible Twos!
Forget the Twos. The Twos are a piece of cake. The Threes, on the other hand…not so pleasant. And don't get me started on the Fours, Fives, and Sixes. Personally, I'm looking forward to the Twenty-fives.

Myth #3: You get used to it.
Whether it's the mess, the lack of sleep, the daily dinnertime stand-offs and bedtime battles, they always tell you that "you'll get used to it

eventually." Horse hockey. The only thing you ever really get used to is a glass or two of Cabernet every night in order to kill the pain.

Myth #2: Parenthood Teaches You to Be Selfless
Not so. If anything, it teaches you to be self-*ish*. What I wouldn't give to be alone somewhere quiet, with a cup of coffee and a good book, and not have to worry about being struck between the eyes at any moment by a stray Nerf bullet.

Myth #1: Parenthood is the greatest thing in the world.
I have to admit, despite the mental exhaustion, ubiquitous mess, and ever-present longing for those glorious days when you were only responsible for one human being, i.e., yourself, parenthood has been one of the best and most rewarding experiences of my life. Honestly, it's pretty darn awesome.

But sorry, parenthood, as far as greatest things in the world go, you'll always come in a close second to cheesy-bacon-ranch fries.

An Open Letter to My Future Children

Dear Kids,

I hope you are doing well in the future, riding around on your hover boards and telepathically texting your friends via your iBrain implants.

Things are great here. You are both still young and cute and don't need to use deodorant yet. Best of all, you still like me.

For example, the other day I was out for a run, and as I was coming out of the cemetery, aka the Beaver Cemetery, Mausoleum and Fitness Center, I saw you guys as Nana was bringing you home. The good Nana she is, she pulled over and waited for me to catch up so I could say hello. When I reached her car, you two had unbuckled from your car seats and were hanging out the window saying, "Daddy! Daddy!"

Then you both kissed me – get this – ON THE MOUTH! You even continued to wave and smile as I went back to my run and you passed me on your way home.

In the future, i.e., where you are now, people keep telling me that you are going to hate me and want nothing to do with me. I hope not, but odds are they're right.

Just remember: YOU are the ones who changed. Not your mother and me. Now if you'll excuse me, I'm going to go give you both a zerbert.

Love,
Daddy

Summer—Season of the Time Suck

On the surface, it sounds like a simple request: "Daddy...can we go swimming?"

But those five little words end up setting off a chain reaction of work and wasted time that can derail even the most disciplined of work-from-homers.

When I embarked on this new and exciting freelance writing journey, I knew I'd have to learn how to deal with the occasional interruption from my kids. Honestly, I was looking forward to it; seeing more of my children was one of the main reasons I wanted to work from home in the first place.

There was just one little thing I didn't account for: summertime.

During the colder months it's easy to keep the kiddos occupied by popping in a DVD or setting up a tent-city in the living room, both of which will buy you at least a couple hours of uninterrupted alone time.

Summer, on the other hand, is a whole different ball game. There are so many outdoor activities to choose from — picnics, roller-skating, going to the park, and, yes, swimming — all of which require mom and/or dad's assistance and supervision.

In other words, distractions.

Swimming is by far the biggest time-suck for a work-from-home parent. We just have a small, plastic kiddie pool. But don't let that fool you. What it lacks in size it makes up for in pain in my butt.

Since we store the pool outside, it's almost always covered with spider webs, and the inside surface is forever coated with some mysterious brown crud. So before any actual swimming can take place, the pool first needs to be thoroughly scrubbed and sprayed. Time-suck.

Next, as the pool is filling with ice-cold water from the hose, I have to get the kids prepared for their polar plunge. First I have to locate their swimsuits, which somehow mysteriously disappear between each use. Then, when I finally locate them, my daughter usually throws a fit and complains that she wants to wear some other swimsuit, which, of course, we left up at Grandma's house last weekend. Time-suck.

Then comes the part I hate the most: the application of the sunblock. Don't get me wrong, it's not that I'm against protecting oneself from the harmful rays of the sun; it's just that I'm against struggling to apply the greasy liquid to my son — aka, The Animal — as he squirms around and keeps asking me over and over if I'm done yet. Major time-suck.

Of course, when you finally do get them nicely coated with sunblock, into their swimsuits, and out the door, you still can't get a lick of work done, because obviously you can't leave them alone in a swimming pool. And every five minutes or so, one of them has to go pee-pee, or they want a snack, or my son's nose is running, or there's an ant in the pool, or one of them has to tattle on the other one for hitting, splashing, spitting, being mean, etc.

And after all that, they end up swimming for a grand total of 7 minutes before they become bored and want to get dried off and dressed.

And guess who has to help with that?

Potty Mouths

So the other evening I'm sitting on the front porch enjoying a book of Billy Collins poetry, when my son, aka The Animal, comes to the window. The following is our conversation:

"Daddy! My poop was green!"

"Did you go poop, buddy? Good job."

"No, just pee. But my poop was green!"

"Oh."

Then he runs out the front door, a baby blanket tied around his neck like a superhero cape, and heads straight for the neighbors' house.

"Hey, guys!" he yells, loud enough for the entire neighborhood to hear. "My poop was green! I can't believe it! IT WAS GREEN!"

My kids are both obsessed with poop for some reason. More the saying of it than the actual doing of it. It's their favorite word by far.

Their favorite song? "Daaaddy's a poopie head! A pee and poopie head!"

Actually, they have a number of different poop-themed names for me:

- Poopie-head Daddy
- Mr. Poop-head
- Daddy Poopie-head
- Poopie-face
- Mr. Poopie-face
- Poopie-face Daddy

And, occasionally...
- Mr. Pee-pee-head.

Sometimes I'll say something like, "How about you clean your room for me?" And they'll reply, "How about I poop on your head?"

Not much of a bargain, if you ask me.

For the most part, I really don't mind all the poop talk. Unless we're out in public, that is. Even then I really don't mind it all that much, but of course I have to act like I do, just to keep up appearances.

At home the only place that poop talk is strictly verboten is the dinner table. It's already gross enough just watching my son eat.

I'm not sure why my kids are obsessed with the "P" word or when this potty-mouth phase of their lives will end. But they sure do laugh a lot when they're saying it. And hearing kids laugh is just about the best thing in the world.

So for now...bring on the poop!

PS: I'm not sure why my son's poop was green. Honestly, it didn't occur to me to ask. When you're a dad, some things are just better left unknown.

A Fishy Situation

"Daddy! Something's wrong with Jolly!" It was the end of a long weekend. I had just given the kiddos a shower and was looking forward to getting both them – and myself – to bed. Just then Boogieface passed the fishbowl and saw her beloved goldfish, Jolly, floating on top of the water.

Uh oh.

In the previous couple of days I had noticed Jolly's water getting muckier and muckier. But cleaning it wasn't exactly high up on my want-to-do list. Now it looked as if my gross negligence had led to the little guy's demise.

Ever since my daughter won the fish at the Midland 4th of July carnival, I'd been waiting for (and somewhat looking forward to) the day when we'd wake up to find it belly up and unresponsive. It's not that I don't like fish. It's just that a goldfish is a slippery slope to bigger and more expensive pets—pets that do things like poop on your rug and gnaw on your remote control.

You see, Boogs has been begging us for a dog for a while now. My wife and I told her she can get one when she turns 10. Of course, when that day actually arrives, I'll present her with another enticing option, a la Monty Hall: would she rather have a puppy now or a car when she's 16. I'll keep using the Let's Make A Deal method until legally she's no longer our responsibility.

Don't get me wrong, I love dogs. I just love other people's dogs a whole lot better. After all, that's why grandparents love their grandchildren so much–at the end of the day they get to give them back.

The problem is, my daughter is still a little too young to maintain the fishbowl on her own, so of course the job got added to Mommy and Daddy's ever-growing list of responsibilities. Without a filter, the water has to be changed every couple of days, otherwise it gets all murky and stinks to high heaven. And after three or four cleanings, I was ready to flush the little bugger down the toilet, dead or alive.

So when we found Jolly floating on his side, I have to admit, a part of me was relieved. But then I saw the sadness in my little girl's eyes, I couldn't help but feel for her.

Darn compassion.

But just when we were certain the little guy was doomed, he flapped a fin and gulped some of the filthy water. Boogieface's eyes lit up. "Daddy!" she screamed. "He's still alive!"

Son of a…

I snapped into action. "All right, first thing we gotta do is get him out of that water—STAT!" (OK, maybe I didn't actually say "STAT." But it makes for better drama.) Moving the fishbowl to the kitchen sink, I grabbed the net, scooped Jolly out and transferred him into a dish of clean water. I thought that alone might do the trick, but at first he didn't look any better. Then, gradually, as I cleaned the fishbowl, the whole time gagging at the smell, Jolly began to improve.

Miraculously, just few minutes later, he was back inside his now clean fishbowl and back to his jolly old self again (i.e., floating underwater and doing pretty much nothing).

Boogieface was ecstatic. "Yay, Daddy!" she said. "You saved Jolly! Daddy saved Jolly!"

So in the end I'm a the big hero and Jolly lives to swim another day. Not a bad way to end the weekend.

Now let's just hope the little bugger kicks the bucket in the middle of the night before I have to clean that nasty fishbowl again.

Skip Like A Man

Working from home certainly has its advantages — a 30-second commute, showering every other day, afternoon naps, etc. But the one benefit I never expected was being able to walk my daughter and niece to and from school every day.

We only live a few blocks from their school, so unless it's pouring down rain or we're in the midst of yet another polar vortex, walking just makes sense. But of course you can't just send a couple first-graders off to fend for themselves (at least that's what my wife tells me). So yours truly gets to play chaperone.

I should point out that during our daily walk there is very little actual walking. I don't know how much time you've spent around first-graders, but a nice leisurely stroll isn't in their nature. They prefer to skip, run, hop — basically anything but walk. It's exhausting just watching them.

Every day it's pretty much the same story: As soon as we step out the front door, both girls — each as cute as a button in their Catholic school uniform — grab my hands and start dragging me down the block. Meanwhile I'm still waiting for that first cup of coffee to kick in.

"Let's skip, Uncle Val!" says my niece.

"Yeah!" says my daughter. "And sing 'We're Off to See the Wizard' again!"

That part is my doing, actually. I don't know what it is, but there's just something about the act of skipping that puts me right smack on the Yellow Brick Road. (Cut me some slack—I grew up with two sisters.) Of course, once you do something that your kids enjoy — i.e., skipping down the street to a song from a musical — you better get used to doing it over, and over...and over again.

Each time we come to a street crossing, "The Rule," according to the girls, is that I have to sprint across the street and pull them along with me. They love this. It always gets them giggling and screaming way too loud for 8 o'clock in the morning.

All the way to school there's more running and jumping and giggling and skipping. The skipping in particular always draws befuddled looks from the other parents driving by. I mean, you'd think they'd never seen a grown man skipping down the street before.

Finally we arrive at school, and I give each of them a kiss and a hug as they make their way into the building. Then I make the return journey back to my house, which, now that I am sans kids, is much more leisurely and far less conspicuous. Six and a half hours later I return for the pick-up, and we get to repeat the entire process, only this time in reverse. It's basically the only exercise I get all day.

Just think: If I hadn't quit my full-time job and set out on my own, I never would have been able to work in my underwear. And, oh yeah, I wouldn't have had the opportunity to walk my girls to school and back every day and experience all the wonderful silliness that goes along with it. Sure, my masculinity has probably taken a hit, with all the public skipping and everything. But that's OK. The girls think I'm funny, and that's all that really matters.

Let's just see how funny they think it is when they're 13 and I'm still right there, skipping alongside.

Doh! Oh, Dear.

"What's the matter with you kids?! What—are you just *too cool* to sing anymore? Is that it?"

It's been 30 years now, but I can still see Mrs. Deelo standing at her piano at the front of the classroom, glaring out at us as she expressed her frustration. I really can't blame her. For years in music class we'd sung so enthusiastically and uninhibited. Then, right around seventh grade, the hormones kicked in and our mouths clamped shut. I'm sorry, but there was no way I was going to be caught dead singing "Edelweiss" in public. That's the kind of thing that can follow you for life.

Mrs. Deelo absolutely loved musicals (still does) and she couldn't understand why anyone else wouldn't share in her passion for the genre. She'd show us scenes from "Singin' in the Rain," "My Fair Lady," "Mary Poppins" and others, and then teach us the songs during class. Far and away her favorite musical was the "The Sound of Music." We must have watched that movie a dozen times, or at least that's how I remember it. "My Favorite Things," "Do-Re-Mi," "So Long, Farewell"—we sang these silly songs so often I thought I'd never get them out of my brain. It took me almost 30 years, but finally I was free.

Then I did something stupid—I showed the movie to my daughter.

Boogieface also loves musicals, you see—"Annie" and "Mary Poppins" being two of her favorites. But after watching both of these at least 100 times apiece, she was itching for something new. So we decided to borrow "The Sound of Music" from the local library to see if she liked it. She did, and, much to my surprise, so did my son. To tell you the truth, I even found it to be somewhat enjoyable after so many years of separation, particularly the looming WWII storyline, which appeals to the history buff in me. (Liesel's not too hard on the eyes, either.)

Since they liked it so much, for Christmas we decided to get them the soundtrack on CD so they can hear their favorite songs anytime they wish. Unfortunately, they wish to hear them ALL THE TIME. No joke. The CD is now on loop inside my car, and the kids insist we listen to it anytime we go anywhere. Over the past few weeks I've heard "Do-Re-Mi" so many times I wake up in the middle of the night singing it in my head. "My Favorite Things," ironically, has now become one of my least favorite things, and I've even caught myself singing my own favorite songs with a British accent.

Take it from me, "Sweet Child O' Mine" really loses its edge when you sing it like Julie Andrews.

I'm worried that it's having physical effects on me, as well. At my daughter's gymnastics class recently, one of the other students whispered to her mother — get this — that she thought I looked like Captain von Trapp! I feel like I'm in an episode of The Twilight Zone.

Of course, I could just put my foot down and refuse to play the CD in the car, as is my right as The Daddy. But I have to admit, there's something undeniably sweet about my seven-year-old daughter singing "Sixteen Going on Seventeen," and my four-year-old son contemplating, through song, how one can possibly "solve a problem like Maria."

We see Mrs. Deelo just about every Saturday upstreet at the cafe, and, of course, she was delighted to hear that her love of the movie has been passed along to another generation. So I guess she won in the end.

I suppose I shouldn't complain, though. I mean, it could be worse. At least they've forgotten about "Let It Go." For now.

The Animal—Five Years In

The other day we celebrated my son's fifth birthday. Boy, time sure does fly by. It's hard to believe that, just five years ago, I still thought I wanted four kids.

Funny how things change.

The following is a quick recap of how we celebrated The Animal's big day:

- Even though we had his official party the day before, we set aside a few more presents for my son to open the morning of his actual birthday. Because heaven knows he needed even more toys just a couple weeks removed from Christmas.

- After we dropped off Boogieface at school, we took The Animal to breakfast so he could have his favorite: the Funky Monkey (think chocolate chips, bananas, fudge sauce, and whipped peanut butter) from Waffles INCaffeinated in Beaver. Or, as my dad calls it, "The Waffle House." (He also refers to the Brighton Hot Dog Shoppe as "The Pancake House.")

- Returning home, I actually did a little work (Yay, me!) whilst my son took in six episodes of "Star Wars: The Clone Wars," his favorite show. And, no, I didn't force him (no pun intended) to like Star Wars. He decided that all on his own. OK, maybe I nudged him a bit.

- When The Animal was finished binge-watching, we did battle on his brand-new Teenage Ninja Mutant Turtle Battroborg, which, according to the manufacturer's description, puts "turtle power" in your hands through "precise katana controller movements." This thing is actually pretty cool. You get to make these Teenage Ninja Mutant Turtle robot thingies fight just by swinging around a sword-handle-shaped remote control. To be honest with you, the whole thing kind of freaks me out. I mean, it can't until the government has a whole army of life-sized remote-controlled Teenage Ninja Mutant Turtles to do their bidding? Who's to say they don't already?

— Next we swung by my daughter's school to take her out of class early so we could all go bowling. Because, you know, priorities.

— After The Animal and I bowled our way to victory over the girls, we hit the arcade, which is basically Las Vegas for little kids. With all the noise and flashing lights, I felt like I was in the slots room at Caesar's Palace. And, much like Vegas, we blew through our money limit faster than you can say "rip-off." Speaking of rip-offs, after earning a bunch of tickets playing games, I actually thought the kids would be able to get something half decent in the arcade store. But apparently all 225 tickets buys you nowadays is a flimsy paddleball, two plastic rings, a balsa wood F-18, a handful of Tootsie Roll Frooties, and a couple monkeys with parachutes you can never repack. Thirty bucks well spent.

— Now that the kids were hungry and all wound up from video games and candy, we thought it would be a good idea to go shopping for school uniform pants for my daughter at Old Navy. I spent the next hour chasing them around the store as they hid in the clothing racks. In hindsight, we probably should have done the mind-numbingly boring activity first.

— Finally we headed home to grab some dinner and spend the rest of the evening assessing the mess and wondering where in the heck we're going to put all these new toys. At least that's what I did. The kids just played and had a great time as usual.

It's good to be young.

Saving Storm Shadow

"Hey, Dadda—what's that?!" Shoot. He saw it. My 1984 G.I. Joe Storm Shadow action figure.

I'd been hiding it inside my desk drawer where I knew it would be safe and where, every now and again, I could catch a glimpse of it and recall those oh-so-wonderful days before things like mortgages, electric bills, and chronic back pain.

"Um…well, that's Storm Shadow," I said. "The dreaded white ninja and personal bodyguard of Cobra Commander himself! He was one of my favorite toys when I was a little boy." (Still is.)

The Animal's eyes were aglow. "Wow!" he said. "Can I play with him?"

"What?" I reacted as if he'd asked to play with a butcher knife. "Oh, I'm sorry, pal. But he's not for playing with." My son stared at me, dumbfounded. "He's over 30 years old," I explained, "and I don't want you, you know, losin' him or anything."

You see, I am quite familiar with my son's work. Case in point: I'd already watched him take my once-pristine Matchbox car collection and transform it into a die cast junkyard. Whoever came up with the phrase "with kid gloves" definitely didn't have him in mind.

Eventually, though, I came to my senses and decided to let him have it. I'm a grown man, for cryin' out loud. I don't need to hang onto some stupid action figure for nostalgia's sake. ("Toy Story 2" was on later that day and it got to me.)

What was the big deal, anyway? After all, Storm Shadow is a toy, and toys are meant to be played with. What's the worst that could happen?

A few days later, my son came up to me holding Storm Shadow's torso in one hand and his legs in the other.

"Um, Dadda...your ninja broke."

"Yes, I see that," I replied, as he handed me the remains of my cherished toy. It had taken The Animal just three days to destroy something that for more than 30 years I had kept in near-perfect condition. Knowing his record, I shouldn't have been surprised.

I was devastated. But I wasn't about to just toss him in the garbage. (Storm Shadow, that is; not my son.) Upon closer examination of the bisected figurine, I realized that the broken rubber band that had been holding him together was exactly the same size as those little multi-colored rubber bands my daughter uses to put her hair up, and which I'm always sucking up with the vacuum. Although I'd never attempted surgery on an action figure before (or on anything else, for that matter), I had to at least try to save my old friend. So I washed up, grabbed my philips-head screwdriver, and went to work.

It was a complicated procedure and one that required the complete disassembly of the once proud ninja warrior. It took about a half hour to thread the tiny rubber band into place and then screw everything back together. When I was finished, my beloved Storm Shadow was as good as new! Or at least as good as a 30-year-old action figure can be.

It was my proudest moment, next to the time I managed to change out the innards of my commode without flooding the house.

Of course, now that Storm Shadow was whole again, there was no way in the world I was going to share the good news with The Animal. I mean, I know toys are supposed to be played with and everything, but I'm also pretty sure they appreciate not being torn in half by rambunctious preschoolers with a history of toy abuse.

Believe you me, Storm Shadow is much happier spending the rest of his life safely inside my desk drawer.

Trust me. I know him better than anyone.

Surrendering to the Mess

That's it. It's over. I surrender. I can no longer keep up with the ever-growing, all-consuming mess of toys that has taken over my once beautiful home and infiltrated every nook and cranny therein. It was a valiant fight, and one that has brought many a gray hair to my head. But sometimes you just have to know when to wave the white flag.

The battle began years ago, as soon as my kids were old enough to crawl. They'd make a mess, usually by emptying out a cupboard or toppling something over, and I'd be right there, following close behind to clean it up. I like things neat and tidy, you see. it just feels good having everything in its place. And, whenever possible, in right angles. And preferably square with the walls.

Clean = good. Messy = bad.

But as my kids got bigger, unfortunately so did the messes. Right as I'd pick up the last LEGO, my son would dump out his Matchbox cars all over the floor. The minute I placed the last of my daughter's stuffed animals back on her bed — in order according to size and height, of course — she'd set up a baby doll tea party right in the middle of the bathroom floor. Lovely.

For years I tried to keep my head above water and manage the mess by disposing of any toy that hadn't been played with over a reasonable period of time—say, six months or so. Whenever the kids weren't looking, I'd fill a cardboard box with these neglected toys and sneak it down to the darkest, scariest room in the basement, hoping they'd never realize their toys were missing. Then, when spring came around, I'd mix the hijacked toys in with all the other junk and hope that someone would take them away before my kids became wise of the situation.

Whatever was left at the end of the day would then be carted off to Goodwill, where it could go forth and clutter someone else's life.

And, you know what? It worked.

For a while.

But then a birthday would come along, or Christmas, and despite our desperate pleas to the parents and in-laws for mercy, a whole new mountain of toys would come flooding through the door to take up residence in the living room and, in turn, send my anxiety through the roof.

In a last-ditch effort for a somewhat-clean home, last year my wife and I decided to move both kids into one bedroom and turn my daughter's old room into a playroom where they could keep all of their toys in one place. All six million of them. (It's a big room.)

But of course, the playroom just became a staging area for their daily mess attacks, and gradually the toys found their way back down the stairs and into the living room, where they'd take up permanent residence and send me stumbling head over heels in the middle of the night on my way to the bathroom.

And it's not just the toys that drive me nuts. It's the pop-up tent cities, made from every blanket and sheet in the house. It's the craft-tastrophies that turn the dining room table into a construction paper killing field. It's the dozens of cardboard boxes, sliced up, shaped, and taped into boats and Box Trolls, caves and cars, spaceships and suits of armor.

There's simply no escaping it!

Therefore, in order to preserve what's left of my sanity and to survive the remainder of these fully-nested years, I've decided to throw in the towel, so to speak, admit defeat, and give in to the mess.

And you know what? It's actually been quite liberating. Sure, my house looks like a garbage dumpster all the time now. But at least I'm not stressing anymore over the little things, like all the little invisible LEGOs buried deep down within the fibers of my living room carpet, waiting to jab an unsuspecting victim right in that oh-so-tender part of their foot.

I just wear shoes indoors now.

So if you happen to stop by my house anytime in…oh, the next decade or so, please, excuse the mess. Because it's staying where it is, right smack in the middle of the living room floor…and in the foyer… and on the kitchen counter…and on the dining room table…and…

Father Goose Fail

I thought about recounting in detail everything that's happened over the past six days, when my sister, brother-in-law, and their four young daughters came in from out of town and stayed with us. But honestly, it was pretty much all one big, chaotic blur.

And, besides, I'm just too tired.

Instead I'll share with you one story that basically sums up the past week of my life...

So my nephew Dane had a baseball game on Monday night, and we all went down to watch him play. Of course it was only minutes before the natives, i.e., my kids and my nieces, became restless, so I decided to take them across the street to the playground. That's right—just yours truly and five kids ages 7, 5, 5, 4, and 3.

Piece of cake.

We hadn't been at the park for more than five minutes before the 4-year-old, my niece Carina, jumped off the swings and came up to me, her hands clutching the front of her shorts.

"Uncle Val, I have to go pee-pee."

Of course she did. Unfortunately the closest port-o-potty was way on the other side of the baseball field.

"Sometimes Daddy lets me go outside," she offered.

"Oh yeah?" I replied. "OK then, let's just go behind that little shed over there." So we walked around the back where we knew no one could see. "All right," I said, "go ahead. Go pee-pee."

But she just stood there looking up at me.

"What's wrong? Can't you do it by yourself?"

She shook her head no. "Daddy usually holds me."

So I crouched down and held her up off the ground so she could do her business. Everything was going just fine…until, suddenly and inconceivably, she straightened her body out, which caused her to pee all over her little Elmo panties and shorts. And my hands.

After I cleaned her the best I could using her own underwear, she took off to go play again and I stood there holding the urine-soaked undies.

A couple minutes passed when the sound of a car alarm broke the air. I turned and looked across the field and saw that it was my car that was making all the racket… because it had just been backed into by a large pick-up truck. Splendid.

"Stay right here!" I told the kids as they climbed around on the jungle gym. "I'll be right back." So, keeping one eye on the kids, I sprinted across the field, the wet underwear still in one hand and my car keys in the other as I frantically pushed the alarm's off button. Of course, this being Beaver, I actually knew the guy who backed into me.

"I'm sorry," he said, looking down at the dent in my hood caused by the tow hitch on the back of his pick-up.

But this was no time to think about exchanging insurance info or anything like that. "It's fine," I said. "Don't worry about it." Then I turned around and took off back across the field to the kids.

By the time I got back to the playground, the skies had turned dark and rain was imminent. So I texted my sister and wife and told them to come over quick if it started to rain. Then, just as the raindrops began to fall, my five-year-old niece Lucia walked up to me.

"Uncle Val, I have to go pee-pee."

Of course she did.

I glanced over at the shed for a moment, then down at the soiled underwear that were still in my hand for some reason, and decided it was time to go.

So as the rain fell, I led my flock back across the field and told the kids to stand against the fence while I ran over to to the port-o-potty to get Lucia settled in. Then the rain started to come down harder, so I ran back over to the kids and herded them all into the back of my freshly dented Sonata. Then I ran halfway back and stood there in the rain, looking back and forth between the car and the plastic outhouse until my niece was finished.

Luckily my sister and wife pulled up just then and saved me before any further catastrophes happened or any of the other kids decided that they had to go pee-pee.

And that was one of the calmer episodes of the week.

Father and Son Time

One of the benefits of working for yourself is that on certain days you can choose not to work, which is what I did last Friday.

It's not that I didn't need to work; it's just that my wife was sick and The Animal had been driving both of us crazy. So I figured the best thing to do was to get him out of the house and see if I could drive him to exhaustion in the unseasonably warm, mid-May heat.

I decided to take him for a bike ride. A very long bike ride. With his little legs pumping at about three times as fast as mine in the thick, humid air, I knew he'd be tuckered and rendered harmless out in no time.

After making our way across town, we took a shortcut through the Beaver Cemetery, aka, the Beaver Cemetery, Mausoleum and Fitness Complex.

"Yes!" he said as we entered the graveyard. "This is my dream!" Then he kicked it into hyper-speed, zooming past the lines of tombstones on his Lightning McQueen-themed mini dirt bike.

Popping out on the other side, we passed through the McDonald's — or "Old McDonald's", as he calls it — parking lot and were heading around the back of the Dollar General, when suddenly I heard a skidding sound followed by a crash. I turned around to see the poor little guy flat on the asphalt, his legs twisted up in the pedals.

Cue the tears.

Fortunately, he's a tough little dude, and I was able to convince him that the large, bloody, gravel-infused gash on his elbow was actually a badge of honor. If it had been my daughter, on the other hand, the ambulance would have shown up already just by following the screams.

Finally we reached Tamaqui park—one of those good, old-fashioned playgrounds featuring the kind of rusty, all-metal equipment that pretty much guarantees you're going to get gashed, burnt, or knocked out cold. There we found another brave 5-year-old named Alex tempting fate on the iron pipe jungle gym.

Immediately The Animal approached him to show off of his fresh and still bleeding crash wound. "If you were in my family," he said to the wide-eyed Alex, "you'd probably die."

Boys really know how to make friends with anyone.

It wasn't long before he grew tired of the swings and the two-rails-with-the-iron-bar-suspended-in-the-middle-by-chains thingamajig, so we jumped on our bikes and rode over to another "new" playground over by the old Vanport school. After spinning him around on the merry-go-round a couple times, I let him go off to play on the tube slide while I sat down and tried not to throw up from nausea.

Since we both had to pee, and since I wanted french fries, we headed back over to McDonald's (Shhh! Don't tell my wife!), where after using the restroom we split a medium fry and enjoyed a couple vanilla cones. I taught him how to dip his french fries in ice cream, and he taught me how to dip them in both ketchup and ice cream.

Don't knock it 'til you've tried it.

On the way back we stopped at Castle Toys & Games to pick up a present for my nephew's birthday, and I bought a little more time for my wife. Meanwhile The Animal played with the toys and trashed someone else's place for a change. (Thanks, Linda!)

By the time we got back home later that afternoon, my wife was feeling better after a few hours of peace and quiet, which is pretty much non-existent in our house these days.

I, too, was feeling great after spending a fun, carefree, work-free afternoon with my little guy. And although he was tired, I think he had a pretty good time as well.

Bloody gashes and all.

Another Lovely Dinner

I knew there was going to be trouble right from the start. "Is this fish or chicken?" asked The Animal, as my wife placed the blue Pyrex on the table.

Uh-oh.

"It's chicken," replied my wife.

"It doesn't look like chicken," Boogieface chimed in. The chicken had paprika on it—a foreign substance to my children.

The Animal grimaced. "Uck. It looks disgusting!"

"That is extremely rude," said Cass. "How would you like it if I told you something you made looked 'disgusting'? Now sit down and eat. We're going somewhere fun after dinner, but only if you finish on time."

She was taking them to the library for a special pajama story time. At least…that was the plan.

Of course, when it was time to leave, everyone had finished their meal except for The Animal, who was trying to bargain his way out of eating his two — yes, two — green beans.

"How 'bout if I just eat my chicken?" he asked, batting his 5-year-old eyelashes at us.

"Sorry. You have to eat everything, buddy," I answered. "And you better hurry up—they're going to leave without you!"

"Just ignore him, Val," said Cass. "He knows what he has to do. If he doesn't finish in time, he's not going. It's that simple."

Cue the tears. "NO, MOMMY! DON'T LEAVE ME!"

I tried urging him along. "Com'on, buddy—hurry up! You don't want to have to stay here with me, right?" Honestly, I was looking forward to the alone time. "Just put the green beans in your mouth and get it over with."

"But I already tried green beans before," he said, sniffling. "And I don't like them!"

"Try them again," said Cass. "The doctor said you have to try something 50 times before you begin to like it."

I wasn't sure about that little factoid, but I didn't want him to miss out on story time. "Com'on, buddy," I said. "Just eat them. They're getting ready to leave!"

But Cass had had enough. "Just forget it, Val," she said. "It's too late. We're leaving."

"NO, MOMMY! NOOOOOOO!!!!"

By this point the little guy was so worked up he was nearly hyperventilating. I could see we were well past the point of reasoning, so I just went to the kitchen to start cleaning up. "Sorry, pal," I said as I rinsed off the dishes. "But you had your chance." I always know the right thing to say.

The Animal, however, was not amused. "I AM GOING, Daddy! And I'm NOT eating my green beans either!!"

I stopped loading the dishwasher, slowly turned, and gave him my I'm-The-Daddy scowl. "You do NOT raise your voice to me—do you understand!?"

By this time Boogieface was already in her PJs and headed out the back door to get her bike. Cass followed close behind. "OK," she said. "We'll see you later."

"MOMMY, NOOOOO! DON'T GO WITHOUT ME!! MOMMY!"

I decided to give him one more shot at it. "Look," I said, walking back into the dining room. "They're leaving. So pick up those green beans and shove them in your mouth—now!"

"But, Daddy…"

"NOW!"

And he did. And then he gagged and threw up right onto his plate.

It was at this point that I realized the irony of the situation. At his age I too despised green beans and would marathon dinner sit-ins at my parents' dining room table. And now, here I was doing the same thing to my own son. I felt terrible.

"It's OK, buddy," I said, picking up his plate. "Just go." And off he went with my wife and Boogs, sniffling and whimpering as he walked out the back door.

Finally, it was over.

Or was it?

A couple minutes later I peered out the back door to the garage and could see Boogieface just standing there with her bike. Cass and The Animal were nowhere to be found.

I opened the door. "What are you doing?" I said. "Where's Mommy and your brother?"

"I can't get Bunny in my bag and he's gonna fall out." Apparently they were told to bring their favorite stuffed animal to the event.

"Just shove him in the bag and get going. You're going to be late. Hurry up—Mommy is waiting for you!"

But once again Cass had had enough. "Forget it," I heard her say as she rolled back into the garage on her bike. "We're not going."

"NO, MOMMY!" Now it was Boogs' turn to cry. "I don't know what to do! Bunny keeps falling out!"

Cass stomped over, grabbed the pink bunny by the head, and shoved him down into my daughter's backpack, which was hanging from the handlebars on her bike. "There!" she said. "Now let's go! Honestly, I don't know why I try to do anything for you kids!"

And so ended yet another memorable dinnertime at the Brkich household. For once I was glad to be doing the dishes alone.

To tell you the truth, with dinners like this, it's amazing any of us can keep our food down.

The Sound of Silence

I'd been dreaming about it for years. The day when both our kids would head off to school and leave me with six and a half glorious, peaceful, kid-free hours to do as I pleased (i.e., work, nap, read, nap again, repeat.). For stay-at-home parents like my wife and me, the first day of school is basically a national holiday. The first day that all of your kids go to school, on the other hand, is like every single holiday wrapped into one.

With unlimited margaritas.

After a surprisingly drama-free breakfast, we took the standard first-day-of-school photo on the front porch before heading off for their school a couple blocks away. Boogieface was excited about the second grade. My son, however, was a little hesitant about starting kindergarten, so we weren't sure how it was going to go. The only thing we were pretty sure about was that the phone calls from his teacher would be coming by the end of the week.

When we got to his classroom, The Animal stopped dead outside the door. "I'm not going in," he said, standing in the threshold, his brand new R2-D2 book bag resting on his back.

Uh, oh, I thought. Here we go.

But then, not two minutes later, he was sitting on the floor with his new friends building a castle, his first-day nervousness a thing of the past.

The kindergarten classroom was alive with activity as the students bounced around and got used to their new surroundings. Meanwhile, parents looked on, some with tears in their eyes, others with wide grins on their faces (guess which one I was).

"Have a great first day, buddy!" I said, giving my boy a big hug and a kiss before walking out of the room singing "Zippity Do Dah!" under my breath. "I'll see you after school."

Six and a half glorious hours from now!

Cassie, not ready to let her little boy go just yet, stuck around a few minutes more and made sure he had all of his supplies ready to go at his desk.

"Com' on!" I mouthed to her from out in the hallway. "Let's go! Before he changes his mind!"

Two years before, when we dropped off Boogieface for her first day of kindergarten, Cassie and I were both overcome with sadness, wiping back tears as we left our little princess behind. But this time, for some reason, it seemed much easier. At least it was for me.

"Aren't you sad," said Cass as we walked back to our house. "Our babies are all grown up."

"Heck no!" I replied. "Good riddance. Just think—12 more years and we'll really be free!" Of course, I was just kidding.

Kind of.

It wasn't 30 seconds after we got home, however, that I noticed how quiet it was. It was eerie. There was no one in the living room playing video games and shouting at the TV. No one up in the playroom making a gigantic mess. No one yelling to me from the other room to get him some more tea. It was so peaceful. So quiet. So unbearably empty. All of a sudden I could feel the tears welling up in my eyes.

What was wrong with me? This is what I had been wishing for. Yet, here I was, devastated and — I can't believe I'm saying this — missing my wild little Animal and all his craziness.

Suddenly six and a half hours seemed like a really, really long time.

Later that afternoon, we walked back to the school. As I stood outside with the other parents, I couldn't wait to see my kids, give them both a big hug, and hear all about their day. Then the principal opened the front door, and I caught a glimpse of The Animal standing inside the lobby. When he spotted me across the street, he beamed and gave me the peace sign, looking like a little Nixon bidding farewell after resigning the Presidency.

Finally they got the go ahead, and he came running out to me as I braced for a long-anticipated, much-needed hug. But then, just as he got close, he slowed to a walk and a frown grew on his face.

"Daddy!" he said, his tone thick with frustration. "That peanut butter banana you gave me for lunch was terrible! It looked just like chocolate throw up!"

And with that, once again I was longing for the silence.

After-School Chaos

You might remember a couple of months back I wrote about how sad I was after sending The Animal off to all-day kindergarten and then returning to my startlingly quiet home. That was the moment I realized how much I'd enjoyed having him around, and the resulting silence left by his departure left me utterly heartbroken.

Well, I got over that pretty quick. Like the next day.

Honestly, it's been quite wonderful having the entire day to myself. Not only has it enabled me to get a ton of work done, but it's also allowed me to catch up on one of my favorite pastimes: napping.

Of course, all good things must come to an end, and this particular good thing comes to an end right around three o'clock every day when I pick up my kids and my niece from school. After spending the majority of my day in relative silence, suddenly I find myself thrust into a world of raving lunatics who are now intent on releasing all that pent-up energy from sitting in school all day long.

After the initial explosion of youthful exuberance that sends them bouncing all over the house, screaming and yelling and pealing off their school uniforms as they go, if I'm lucky I manage to get them to pause long enough to do their homework. Unfortunately, this just opens up a whole 'nother can of worms. This ain't your mama's homework, you see. Boogieface, for example, is only in the second grade, yet her math homework looks like it was drawn up by Stephen Hawking. For a wordsmith like me, who prefers to avoid numbers at all costs, it can be especially confusing. I mean, do we really even need math anymore? Personally, I'm surviving just fine without it.

The Animal usually just has a single page he has to color. Now that's my kind of homework. But the girls usually have a whole page of math and another whole page of writing/grammar, plus a story they have to read aloud to me from their reader. The 30 minutes to an hour that it takes for them to complete their homework is one filled with so much moaning and whining, sometimes I feel like I'm the overseer of a medieval dungeon—albeit one with a bunch of LEGOs all over the ground.

I don't know about you, but I don't ever remember having homework that was so lengthy and difficult that I needed to ask my parents for help. And definitely not when I was in second grade. I mean, what's the point of making it though grades 1-12, not to mention four more years of college, if you have to relive it all over again through your children? If I would've known that, I'd have waited until I had children to begin my academic career.

After homework the kiddos always beg me for an after-school treat, which I flatly deny because a) dinner's not that far off and b) I know they didn't eat half of the lunch I packed them earlier that morning. If I'm lucky and it's a nice day out, I can convince them to go outside to play so that I can enjoy a few more moments of peace before the Battle of Dinnertime begins.

However, that doesn't always go so well either.

Like the other day, when after convincing them to go outside, I headed into what Sr. Margaret used to refer to as the "lavatory." Surely the kids would be fine on their own for a few minutes. But just moments later I heard the screen door slam and my daughter yelling that her brother was hurt. "Come quick, Daddy!" she said. "He got hurt, and his eye is bleeding!"

I panicked, of course, imagining the worst as I hastily made myself… well, presentable. Right then he came inside, crying hysterically, several fresh red gashes across his face. Apparently he had run straight into some thorns, or what we in Western PA call "jaggers." Luckily he was more afraid than anything and his eye hadn't been harmed. Whew.

Maybe having such a large portion of the day all to myself isn't such a good thing after all, considering it just sets me up for such a shock later on when school lets out. Then again, maybe I just need to learn how to embrace the chaos.

That and take longer naps during the day. I need the energy later on.

The Last Times

Parents are always marking their children's "firsts." The first time they roll over. The first word they speak. The first time they walk. The first time they have an explosive, diaper-overflowing bowel movement when you're at the mall, you don't have any diapers, and you just used your last wipey. (True story.)

These are all memorable moments, make no mistake about it. But whenever my kids cross one of life's milestones, I can't help but think that it also signifies the end of something. My wife would say this is an example of my glass-half-empty personality. (In my opinion, there's only two types of glasses: full and not full. Especially when it comes to wine.)

But I think it's more than that.

We're always looking ahead to the next thing, whether it's with our kids or in our lives. And although there's nothing wrong with planning for the future and working towards a goal, I think we have to be careful not to miss what's happening today, right now. Sometimes we're so focused on when our kids have another "first" in their life, we fail to recognize that it also marks the last time for something else.

As I go through this crazy adventure of parenthood, I wish I knew when a "last" was about to happen, just so I knew to pay attention. Because, looking back, there are so many things they used to do — some good, some not so much — that passed by without me even realizing it.

I wish I could remember…

The last time she crawled over to me.
The last time he sat in his high chair at dinner.
The last time I changed her diaper.
The last time he peed in my face.
The last time I laid her in her crib.
The last time I buckled him into his car seat.
The last time I listened for her breathing over the monitor.
The last time I played airplane with his broccoli.
The last time I panicked because we lost her binkie.
The last time I fed him a bottle.
The last time I caught her at the bottom of the slide.
The last time he scooched down the steps on his bum.
The last time she had a meltdown because her sock felt "weird."
The last time I held him in just one arm.
The last time she played with that old "favorite" toy.
The last time he watched Sesame Street.
The last time she used my belly like a trampoline.
The last time he asked me to push him on the swings.
The last time I pushed them to the cafe in the stroller.

One day, not too long from now, they'll graduate from high school and move out of my home forever (well, hopefully), and it will mark the last of the "lasts." So for now, I'm going to do my best to pay attention and hope that it's still a long, long time before the last time I carry them upstairs to bed…the last time they ask me to take them to the park…the last time they actually want to spend time with me.

Because, you know, all these "lasts" won't last forever.

Keeper of the Doodles

"This is for you, Daddy," says The Animal, handing me a piece of paper featuring his latest work of art—a blue-headed monster/demon, with a yellow body and orange arms, and which is surrounded by 19 stamped monkeys and two (what I assume are) stars. If anyone else had handed this to me, I'd have crumpled it up and tossed it (and most likely suggested mental help). But since it's my son's creation, I hang it on the fridge for a couple weeks before dating it and then putting it in a box in the basement. It's just what I do.

When you're a parent, as soon as your kid is old enough to put crayon to paper, you earn the title of Official Childhood Archivist. Suddenly you find yourself saving all of your child's indecipherable doodles and scribbles as if he or she was a miniature Rembrandt. Nonsensical blobs, preposterous portraits, and other pieces of Crayola crap, that normally you'd toss in the trash, are instead dated and displayed on your refrigerator for a while before being preserved for posterity.

When I was a kid, I was always doodling something: spaceships… dinosaurs…spaceships attacking dinosaurs, etc. Most of the time I did this while in school, where I was bored out of my gourd. Luckily my mother had the foresight to preserve these works of art so that I am able to enjoy them today. Just think, without her tireless efforts, future generations would have been robbed of things like this:

I like to joke with my mother that she's a hoarder. Of course, I know that's not true. I mean, she doesn't have a single cat. That said, I'm so grateful that she held onto these early pieces of my creative development. It's so cool to be able to see things that I drew oh-so-many years ago, long before the weight of the world fell upon me, crushing my spirit and extinguishing my once vivid imagination. One day, when my kids become adults and, like me, lose their enthusiasm for life, I'd like them to have something they can pull out of that box in the attic and say, "What the hell is this?"

Boogieface tends to draw things like fairies, butterflies, and flowers. The Animal focuses on three main categories: monsters, robots and anything Star Wars. Hers are usually sweet and pretty (see Exhibit A). His can be violent and sometimes downright frightening (see Exhibit B). Hers might actually be worth something one day when she becomes a famous artist. His most likely will be studied by psychiatric specialists and members of law enforcement.

Of course, as my kids have gotten older, I've become more discerning about what to keep and what to toss. When my daughter was younger, we'd keep every single piece of cra…I mean art that she created. But I soon learned that if we kept up this exhaustive process, we'd quickly run out of space in the Archives, a.k.a., the basement. Therefore I've become a little more selective about what we to save. Picture of an X-Wing Fighter attacking an army of aliens? Keep. That cookie-cutter, paper-hand turkey they made at school? Toss.

When it comes to being an archivist, you have to be able to make the tough decisions.

And childhood archiving doesn't end with their hand-drawn art. It also includes the thousands upon thousands of blurry, digital photos you take of them at their Christmas pageants, on vacation, in the living room, etc., which then clog up your hard drive; those old shoes and pieces of clothing you just can't bear to throw away, even though they smell like garbage; and those former-favorite toys that you'd thought they'd play with forever until their next favorite toy came along. It's time-consuming. It's overwhelming. It's exhausting. But trust me, one day they'll appreciate it.

Then it will be up to them to figure out where to store all that crap.

The End of The Raggies

"Oh great, what now?" I thought, hearing a thud from upstairs. I had just put the kiddos to bed and sat down in the den with a good book and a better beer. Now one of them was up, and it was only a matter of time until he or she came downstairs. Wonderful.

Just then the door opened and Boogieface walked in. "What's wrong, baby?" I asked, expecting her to say that either her brother was being too loud or that — big surprise! — she wasn't tired.

But then she reached out and shocked the you-know-what out of me.

"Here," she said, holding out her beloved Raggies. "There's no room in my bed for these anymore. And look—they're all ripped and falling apart."

Her Raggies were actually cloth diapers/burp cloths from when she was born. In time they became her nightly companions, without which she couldn't sleep. There's probably been a dozen or so times when, during a sleep over at the in-laws', we'd get a late-night call saying that Boogs had forgotten her Raggies at home, and then I'd have to make the 10-mile trek to deliver the sleep-inducing cloths. She loved those things.

Yet, here she was, handing them over to me as if they meant nothing to her.

I tried to hide my emotion as I sat there holding the tattered, once beloved pieces of cloth. "I'll take care of them," I said. "How about we put them downstairs in your memory box?" She smiled and nodded, and then feigned a frown as she bid her nighttime friends adieu forever and went back upstairs to bed.

I sat there, stunned. Devastated. I mean, you never think about things like this until they happen. And when they do, it completely rips your heart out.

I knew this moment was coming months ago when she first showed us her rapidly disintegrating Raggies. Of course, I wasn't just going to sit by idly and let this integral part of her life just fade into history. So I went online and scoured the Internet, trying to find out where and from whom we had originally purchased these burp cloths eight years earlier. But with no tags and no idea of the manufacturer, it was like looking for a needle in a haystack.

Finally, after a couple weeks of searching (I'm not kidding) I stumbled upon what looked like the same type of cloths on an Etsy page. I couldn't find the exact same pink leopard and pink-and-green polka dot designs of her original Raggies, but I was able to find some other designs that I hoped — and prayed — she would like just as much.

On Christmas morning, I handed Boogs the wrapped up cloths and hoped for the best. But as she opened the gift, her reaction was lukewarm at best. Oh, well. Maybe it really was time to move on.

But then, a couple of days later, she mentioned to me that she had been sleeping with her new Raggies and that they were starting to get all soft and cuddly, just like her other ones. Success! The Raggie Era and this innocent, oh-so-precious time of my baby girl's childhood had been extended. At least for a little while longer.

So there I was, sipping a beer and staring at the tattered remains of my daughter's once beloved Raggies, my heart broken. How could I possibly take them down to that dark, cold basement and leave them there in that lonely plastic bin, not to be seen or thought of again for years? I'm sorry, I can't. I just can't.

Maybe I'll just hang onto them a little while longer. You know, keep them at my desk, where I can see them everyday. Heck, maybe I'll even sleep with them myself. What? You've never seen a grown man sleep with a couple cloth diaper/burp cloths before?

The thing is, I was just sitting there trying drink my beer and enjoy a good book. Leave it to life to come out of nowhere and punch me right in the gut when I least expect it.

At least I have something to wipe away the tears.

3 O'Clock Madness

Whenever I see a young family struggling to get through those oh-so-trying early years with their children, I always do my best to encourage them and tell them to just hang in there. After all, before they know it those days of endless diaper changes and sleepless nights will be a thing of the past as their kids grow up and head off to school.

And then it will get much worse.

Don't get me wrong, school is definitely a blessing for the stay-at-home parent. Then 3 o'clock rolls around and all hell breaks loose.

I remember how I was actually tearful when my kids first went off to school. How would I ever get through the day without them? The house was going to be so lonely, so terribly quiet!

HA! What a laugh. It only took a few hours before I learned to embrace — and LOVE — that beautiful, quiet window between 8 a.m. and 3 p.m., when I can actually work, read, and most important, nap, without being disturbed.

But of course, all good things must come to an end, and this particular good thing ends the minute my kids and niece walk through the door. Actually, they don't really walk through the door. It's more like an explosion. They burst in like a gang of violent criminals in a home invasion. Because basically that's what it is.

From this moment on, it's virtually impossible for me to think, let alone get any work done. Heck, my son and niece are already pushing and kicking and tackling each other before they've even gotten out of the foyer. They're a dangerous combination, those two. Apart, they're pretty much harmless, like a match and a stick of dynamite. But put them together and — BOOM! — you've got one volatile combination.

I mean, you'd think they just got released from prison, the way they carry on. Usually they head straight for the kitchen to raid the cupboards, ravenous because they barely ate any of the food they packed for lunch that day. Believe me, I know. I've worked the lunch hour at their school many times, and I can tell you that very little actual eating goes on. Screaming, yelling, bouncing, jumping, laughing—yes. But eating? Not so much.

If I somehow manage to escape back to my desk once my kids get home, it's just one interruption after another. One of them will come in, tears in his or her eyes, claiming that one of the other ones was "looking at them" or something terrible like that. Then, after I send them on their way, another one will come in to defend him- or herself, adamantly claiming their innocence. Again, I'll send them on their way, only to be interrupted again minutes later because someone is touching someone else who doesn't wish to be touched, someone is not sharing his or her toy, or, the most common complaint, someone is "being mean."

Fortunately I only have to experience this 180 days of the year.

So here's the part where you all chime in and tell me I better "cherish these days" and that one day I'll "miss it all." Yeah. Thanks for the tip. By the way, if any of you out there are feeling nostalgic for the good ol' days when your kids were young, just say the word and I'll bring mine over for a visit.

How's 3 p.m. work for you?

Watery Woes

So the other day my in-laws got back from vacation, and they brought the kids back these really cool drinking glasses that flash and light up. The next morning during breakfast I thought it would be fun to fill the glasses up with water and then turn out the lights. Sorta like an early morning disco party, just without the Bee Gees or those terrible outfits.

Boogs got dressed and came downstairs first, and she was really enjoying the light show on the ceiling. The Animal followed a couple minutes later, and he was smiling ear to ear as he walked into the dining room and saw the glasses flashing in the darkness. Then he walked over to his seat, picked up his flashing glass, and, inexplicably, turned it completely upside down, spilling its contents all over the table and all over my wife's work notebooks and other random papers she had left on the table.

"OH, NO!" I cried, scrambling in vain to save the now soaking-wet papers. "Mommy's work!! Why did you do that?!?"

The Animal was in shock. "I didn't know it was full! I didn't know it was full!" he said, as he began to bawl uncontrollably. Just then Cass walked into the room to witness the watery devastation. Luckily she handled the situation much more calmly than I had and comforted our son while I did my best to clean up the mess.

OK, maybe I shouldn't have freaked out like I did. But how you can pick up a full glass of water and not realize that it's full, I'll never know. Kids. Go figure.

Flash forward to today…

Just as I sit down at my desk to do some work, my lovely wife brings me my daily vitamins and a glass of water. Minutes later, I take the vitamin, and as I go to lift the glass of water I catch the corner of the shelf on my desk, knocking the glass out of my hand and spilling its contents all over my desk, my mouse, my keyboard, my papers, etc.

Now I'm sitting here writing this surrounded by damp, wrinkly papers and an oh-so-pleasant pulpy smell constantly reminding me of my clumsiness.

If my wife had been standing here, she would've said, gleefully, "See what you get."

I don't know what, if anything, all this means, other than that the males in this household apparently have a slight drinking problem.

Take Your Kid Nowhere Day

So they tell me today is "Take Your Kid to Work Day." This actually worked out well, since my kids didn't have school today. (Actually, I think that may be the reason they didn't have school today.) Anywho…

Considering that my so called "place of work" is also my "place of sleep," "place of watch Netflix in my underwear," "place of pour myself another IPA," etc., my kids don't get to experience all the fun of normal places of work, such as offices, construction sites, and what have you. Too bad. I think they'd really get a kick out of a 2:30 staff meeting.

Here's what they've gotten to experience so far at Daddy's workplace today:

- From 8 a.m. 'til around noon, they vegged-out on the couch watching cartoons while I was in my "office" (the den) working on a book ghostwriting project. I figured they wouldn't get much out of watching me stare at my computer and tap the keys on my keyboard. Even though, that's basically all I do.

- After that they went to visit Mommy's "place of work", her office up on the third floor. Meanwhile, it being a dreary, rainy day, I put Radiohead on shuffle and enjoyed a brief moment of solitude.

- Five minutes later (told you it would be brief), The Animal rumbled back downstairs and handed me a picture he drew of a giant Pikachu (Pokémon) sitting on a skyscraper and playing an electric guitar. Oh, and he's being attacked by a helicopter-ish gunship thingy.

- Eventually everyone gathered in the lunchroom (our dining room) for a nutritious meal consisting of buttered noodles. The cafeteria here is awesome!
- After that, Mommy went back up to her office, whilst the kiddos and I brought a bunch of Star Wars spaceships down from the playroom and had a pretty sweet battle in the conference room (the living room).
- Now, since it's quitting time (3:30 p.m.), I'm going to pour myself another cup of coffee and go play checkers with Boogieface in front of the fireplace. After that I'll probably take a nap.

'Cause that's how we roll here at Val Brkich Inc. Sorry, we're not currently hiring.

Save the Drama for Your Mama

I can't deal with drama. This is a problem, since I live with the drama queen of all drama queens.

Like most men, I never really understood women. (If you want me to do something, why don't you just ask me to do it?!) When my daughter was born, I thought that maybe since I'd be spending so much time with her, she might actually be the first one that made any sense to me.

Boy, was I wrong.

Last night we were rushing out of the house for soccer practice when Boogs went to fill up her bottle of water. Instead of the normal tap variety, however, she decided she wanted to bring along some flavored, carbonated water. So she asked me to open up the bottle of carbonated water for her so that she could then pour it into her own bottle. The thing is for some reason my wife told her that she couldn't put the carbonated water in another bottle because it might explode from all the shaking. (Huh?) Oh well, whatever. We didn't have time to discuss the laws of science.

Anyway, we finally start heading out the door when Boogs says something about how she can't believe she has to carry this whole big bottle of carbonated water with her. So, trying to be a nice daddy, I take the bottle back to the kitchen and pour some of it in her normal water bottle, leaving enough room in it to prevent any type of "explosion." Then I went back to the front door.

Immediately upon seeing what I did, my daughter, who just seconds before was all smiles, inexplicably breaks out into tears. "I didn't tell you pour it in that bottle!" she cries. "I don't know why you did that!" She then storms out the front door and goes off to pout in the car.

What just happened here?

Anyways, it was a silent, tension-filled ride to the soccer field, where Boogs went running off to her team, bottle of carbonated water in hand.

Fortunately there was no explosion.

Holding Down the Fort

Well, once again I've made it to my favorite time of day, when the kiddos are finally in bed, and I'm on the couch, remote in one hand, glass of vino/beer/brandy/tequila in the other.

Over the past five days, the Mrs. has been been away in Atlanta for a design conference. For the most part, the kids have been great. But when you're the only one getting them up, making them breakfast, packing their lunches, taking them to school, picking them up from school, making them dinner, cleaning up after dinner, taking them to soccer, giving them showers, reading them a book, and then putting them to bed…well, let's just say it's a long day.

God bless all you single moms and dads out there. Seriously, you deserve a medal.

Today we went to 9:15 Mass, and I was really looking forward to the children's liturgy. This is where they take the kids elsewhere during the first and second readings, the gospel reading, and the sermon, giving me at minimum a good 15 minutes of alone time. And, of course, Father forgot about it, which meant an additional 15 minutes of The Animal squirming around in pew and climbing all over me like a capuchin monkey on Red Bull. Because, you know how much 6-year-old boys just love church.

By the time we got to the final blessing, I was counting down the seconds until breakfast at the Hot Dog Shoppe. That's when my son decided to drop the fold-away kneeler directly onto my shins. Oh joy. It probably wouldn't have been any easier if my wife had been there. But at least I would've had someone to share the misery with.

The kids love it when Daddy's in charge, of course. A popsicle before dinner? Sure! Another TV show? Why not?! You wanna go to church in the same pants you slept in? I don't see why not. The way I see it, whatever makes my life easier is A-OK with me.

Another problem being the solo parent is that you've only one set of eyes and one set of ears. For example, the other night at the restaurant, The Animal ordered a root beer, and for some reason the waitress brought him a large, adult size drink. I wasn't paying attention as he sucked it down before his meal came, or when the waitress inexplicably asked him if he wanted another. So by the time his meal showed up, he was already buckled over in the booth with a stomachache. Although this was an obvious parent fail on my part, it actually turned out to be a good lesson as to why we don't normally let them drink pop. So in the end I guess my laissez-faire parenting style turned out to be pretty effective.

Point: me.

My wife is coming home tomorrow evening, so all I have to do is make it through one more day. Boy, are these kids in for a rude awakening. Personally, I'm just looking forward to a nap. I think I earned it.

Summertime...and the Livin' Ain't Easy

Ah, summertime! The long, warm days! The weekend BBQs! The kids coming inside to tattle on each other every five minutes and argue who gets which lightsaber!

I admit it. I was so looking forward to the end of the school year. I was tired of making lunches. I was tired of helping with homework. Mostly I was just tired, and I couldn't wait to sleep in past 6:30 a.m. The thing is, I forgot that when school is out, the kids are always around. Emphasis on always. And when you're a work-from-home writer like myself, this can get old pretty darn quick.

The first couple weeks of summer vacation we were actually on vacation, road-tripping throughout the Southeast and visiting my sister in Florida. You would think that being stuck inside my Hyundai with the kids all day and then at night in the hotel for two whole weeks would've been a taxing experience. But it turned out to be a wonderful time and the kids were very well-behaved. (I can't say the same about myself.)

Then we got back home, and it was back to the daily grind, so to speak. This is when the trouble began.

The first couple hours of the morning are great. I get up around 7:30, 8-ish, go for a nice run, and then enjoy a cup of coffee on the porch before heading to my desk to begin the day's work. Meanwhile, my wife goes up to her office to work, my son chills out on the sofa watching cartoons, and my daughter sleeps in until 10:30 or so. It's a quiet, peaceful type of morning that is very much different than the rushed and chaotic mornings of the school year.

Unfortunately, we can't just let them sleep and watch TV all day long (Can we?), so we tell them to turn off the tube, get some breakfast, do their chores, and then get the heck outside, where, hopefully, they will leave my wife and I alone to get some work done.

Yeah, right.

Take today, for example. Everything seemed to be going smoothly as the kids went outside to play with their lightsabers and toy guns. Next thing I know, The Animal comes back in the house and into my office, bawling because his sister took one of his beloved cap guns when it was his intention to play with both of them.

After summoning Boogieface into the house and trying unsuccessfully to arbitrate the toy-gun situation, I gave up and told them to go off and settle it by themselves (a favorite tactic of my wife's which almost never works).

There was more fighting and whining and crying, of course, but I did my best to ignore it and continue hacking away at my daily workload.

Next thing I know the toy-gun fiasco is over and the two of them are on the front porch playing LEGOs like best friends. Kids—go figure. The peace, however, did not last. Minutes later my son once again comes in crying to me. "Daddy...[sniff, sniff] I went to her pet store [sniff, sniff] and I wanted to buy the fox [sniff, sniff] but she wouldn't let me buy the fox!"

How tragic.

Once again I try to intervene. "Com'on, Boogs, can't you just let him buy the fox for goodness sake?"

"But, Daddy!" she cried. "The fox isn't for sale—he's my pet!"

Seeing that the situation is hopeless, once again I just try to ignore it and go back to work. But the arguing and crying continues until I can take no more. Suddenly I'm stomping out on the porch and making outlandish proclamations:

"That's it! I've had it! The two of you aren't allowed to play with each other anymore!" Then I send them to different sides of the porch and stomp back into the house, dreaming of the good old days (three weeks ago) when I actually had a little peace and quiet.

Gradually things do quiet down and I can hear the kids whispering to each other as they go back to playing nicely. Then I hear another kid's voice. Then another. Our house, you see, has become the de facto meeting place for all the neighborhood kids, thanks in part to the box of old lightsabers I won on some local online auction. So now everyday there's a huge, neighborhood Jedi battle in my yard. And, honestly, I don't really mind.

I am a little jealous, though.

Yes, summer can be a trying time for stay-at-home moms and dads. Still, I'd still rather deal with all the interruptions and crying and mess than try to figure out some inexplicable second grade math problem.

Solo camping in Maine would be even better.

(Robot) Doggone It!

All my daughter wants for Christmas is this stupid robotic dog named "Chip" that, supposedly, you can teach to do obey you and do tricks like fetch a ball. (Yeah, I'm sure that's exactly what it does.) It's definitely not cheap, but at least it doesn't make a mess on the living room carpet.

So last week Boogieface writes a note to Santa asking for the robot dog. She then gives the letter to our Elf on the Shelf, Snowflake (don't even get me started on that) to deliver to the jolly old man himself. In the meantime, my wife goes online and places an order with Amazon Claus.

A few days later, I'm sitting at my computer in the late afternoon when I hear the doorbell. I get up to see who it is and see "Santa" walking down off the porch and back to his big brown truck in the street. When I open the door, I am aghast at what I see. Not a plain brown cardboard box, but a box just like you'd see in the toy store, with big pictures of Chip the robot dog splattered all over it! Luckily Boogs and The Animal had left just minutes before to go spend the night with my in-laws. Otherwise, Lucy, I'd have a lot of 'splainin to do.

Instead of taking the box straight down to the basement to hide with the other gifts, however, I place it on the living room couch where I plan to open it up and test it out first. Unfortunately, I totally forget about it, just as I totally forget about moving our elf from the spot in the kitchen where the kids had last seen him. (Can you see where this is going?)

The next day Cassie and I go Christmas shopping and come home just in time for me to go pick up the kids from school. I have a chiro appointment that afternoon, so after picking up the kiddos I just pull into the drive and tell them to go inside where my wife is waiting for them. Seconds later I get a text:

SHE SAW IT! I'M SHAKING!!!

Saw it? I think. She saw wha—OH NO! I immediately reply, my heart pounding:

JUST MAKE SOMETHING UP! TELL HER IT'S A GIFT FOR SOMEONE ELSE!!

I can't believe it. My daughter's Christmas surprise is about to be ruined and the whole Santa thing is about to be ruined for both of my kids, all because I forgot to hide the damn robot dog, which Amazon inexplicably sent to us in such transparent packaging!

Luckily, my wife and I quickly devise a plan. She'll just tell Boogieface that the robot dog was delivered to us by accident and that Daddy has to take it back to the Post Office so they can send it to the right person. Thankfully, my daughter buys it. Whew! When I get home, I pretend like I'm taking the box out to my car, but I really just hide it in the other room until I can take it downstairs later on.

As for the elf I had forgotten to move, Cassie manages to grab it and toss it across the kitchen to another spot just before the kids come looking for it. Yet another crisis is averted.

Look, I love Christmas and the joy it brings to my still-young (and clearly gullible) children, but, man…it sure is stressful at times.

Elf in a Jar

Today was a landmark day in the history of our Elf on the Shelf, i.e., Snowflake. That's because, for the first time ever, Snowflake left the house.

Oh, sure, he leaves every Christmas Eve (when I gleefully shove him back into the cupboard in the basement) before magically reappearing the day after Thanksgiving (when I go down to the basement and pull his scrawny little elf butt out of the cupboard again).

But today was different. Today Snowflake actually left our house before Christmas, and he did so crammed inside a mason jar so that he could be my daughter's show-and-tell item.

Here's how this momentous day in our elf's, ahem, life came about…

My kids have never actually touched Snowflake, you see. That's because, for those of you lucky enough not to already know this, you can never, ever, touch your Elf on the Shelf, lest he lose his magical power, and therefore not be able to report back to Santa Claus, which, sadly, is the Elf on the Shelf's one and only purpose in life. Just to be safe, every night when I have to move the stupid doll to a new location, I always put it somewhere way up high so that my kids — mainly The Animal — won't be tempted to touch it.

I'm not even sure why I care, really. Having our elf lose its magical powers would surely make my life a whole lot simpler.

Anyway, each Elf on a Shelf's behavior is different because parents all have different traditions and rules. For example, all my wife and I do is move our elf to a different hiding space every night and leave it at that. Other parents, however — parents with way too much extra time and energy — do all sorts of funny, cute little things with their elf, which they then document out on Pinterest and share with the world via Facebook, so that the rest of us can see just what terrible, lazy parents we really are.

Honestly, I'm perfectly fine with that. I've been called a lot worse things than "lazy."

So my sister-in-law comes up with the bright idea to have her daughter's elf hide inside a mason jar so that my niece can then bring it around to places with her, such as to school. Of course my daughter sees this and wonders why we can't do the same thing with Snowflake. Thanks a lot, Sis.

So last night Boogs writes a note to Snowflake and leaves it on the dining room table, where he will be able to see it from where he was at the moment, dangling from the chandelier above:

Said the note, "If you want to go to school with me can you get in the jar? I will not take you out."

Then, a post-script:

"Sorry if that sounded harsh. Can you breathe in this jar?"

Personally, I didn't want to set a precedent and allow the elf outside of our house. But my only other option would have been to pen a response from Snowflake, which I really didn't want to do, considering it would most likely lead to nightly questions, to which yours truly would be required to respond in writing, since the stupid elf has no hands to write with.

So this morning Boogieface comes running down the steps and is thrilled to see her beloved elfin pal tightly sealed inside an air-tight glass jar. Personally, I think it's a little disturbing. But what do I know?

"I'm pretty sure he can breathe," she reassures me, "since he used to be a toy and toys don't really need to breathe anyway." Oh, I see.

She may be naïve, but she sure is cute!

Before we leave for school, Boogs places the jar containing her elf inside a padded case and then carefully carries him out to the car. The whole time I'm thinking, please oh please don't let her drop that thing in school. Otherwise I'll probably be called down to perform some type of Elf on the Shelf emergency rescue mission, which would really throw a wrench in my day.

Then again, it might actually make for an interesting blog post.

They Tell Me I'll Miss All This Someday

Chinese water torture. That's the most accurate way I can describe what it's like having two, sometimes three kids, fresh out of school, all hopped up after sitting in class all day, coming home and invading what for the previous seven hours had been a quiet, peaceful sanctuary.

It's actually kind of nice, at first, to see and hear their youthful exuberance as they bounce from room to room, laughing and screaming and yelling along the way. Having this kind of youthful energy in a home is good for the soul.

For a while.

It doesn't take long, though, for one's appreciation of their youthfulness to dwindle, especially when one is trying to write, read, or maybe even take one's daily afternoon nap.

It always amazes me how just a few of these diminutive yet spirited creatures, when playing who-knows-what in the room directly above you, can sound exactly like a stampeding herd of wildebeests. I mean, the noise! How do I even put it into words? All that laughing and screaming and bouncing and yelling blends together in a fingernails-on-a-chalkboard/dentist-drill/sledgehammer-on-a-spike kind of cacophony that no closed door and no amount of volume on one's radio can prevent from finding and penetrating one's ear canals.

After just 15 minutes of this, the initial drip, drip, drip of their youthful energy begins to feel like the pound, pound, pound of a ball-pine hammer on one's skull.

The problem is, there is no escape. Through some inexplicable twist of fate, I have been made responsible for the safety and wellbeing of these little cherubs (at least from 3-5pm), and it would not be proper for me to do what I'd really like to do, which is to run out the front door, jump in my car, and race to the nearest tavern, where I might calm my frazzled nerves with an ice-cold IPA or two.

But of course, if I did that I'd get arrested and thrown in jail. And that wouldn't be good.

A lot quieter, for sure. But definitely not good.

I Spy with My Little Eye

So it's Super Bowl Sunday and the fam and I, as is our annual tradition, are chillin' (more like boiling) in our friends' hot tub before the big game.

Now, my wife, Boogieface, and I all understand and appreciate the true purpose of a hot tub: relaxation. The Animal, however, sees it as his very own private mini swimming pool and is flopping around the 6x6 tub like a lunatic sea otter.

In an effort to get him to sit still and quit splashing us in the face, I initiate a game of "I Spy," selecting something I know will be almost impossible to find, just to keep the boy occupied and, most important, motionless for a few minutes.

After about five minutes of blissful non-movement on his part, my son chooses to give up the search so that he can take a turn at spying something.

"I spy with my little eye..." he says, "something...brown!"

Meanwhile the rest of us begin to fire out our guesses.

"The barn!"

"That tree!"

"The pile of wood over there!"

No, no, and no. Then, before we can guess again, my son interjects, "Wait, wait, wait. I'm not really sure what it is yet."

"What do you mean you don't know yet?" I ask. "How can you not know?"

"Well," he says, "I was gonna pick one of the branches on that tree way over there, but then I couldn't decide which one, so I just decided to pick something else."

By this time we're all laughing, as my son tries again. "I spy with my little eye…something…blue!"

"The sky!"

"That cooler over there!"

"The bird house!"

Again, no, no, and no.

Says the boy, "It was that blue Ford F-150 we saw on the road on the way here."

By this point I'm beginning to suspect he doesn't understand the rules of the game. "How in the heck are we supposed to find something you saw a half an hour ago, miles down the road?"

The Animal, however, is undeterred. "OK, OK," he says. "I have another one."

By this point we're all pretty much done with the game. But the kid's on a roll.

"OK, I have something. But," he adds, "it's not in this world!"

"What do you mean?" says my wife, by this point crying with laughter. "Is it in another dimension or something?"

He continues. "And…it's white!"

Then, before any of us can venture a guess, he asks us if we want to know what it is. Sure, why not?

"George Washington's hair!"

Of course it is.

So we all laugh a little more and accept that the game is a bust. But, hey, it kept the kid still for a few minutes.

Thank heaven for small mercies.

Field Trip Fun

For anyone who might be interested, here's a brief recap of my recent experience as a chaperone for my son's first-grade class on their field trip to see Disney on Ice:

- 8:05 a.m. — I don't actually need to be at the school until 8:15, but I figured I'd just stick around after dropping the kids off.
- 8:27 a.m. — OK, what's the holdup? I knew I should've brought coffee.
- 8:45 a.m. — After a brief delay, we finally get in line to board the bus to Pittsburgh. For a moment I consider using the restroom before hitting the road, but then the line starts moving so I decide against it.
- 8:55 a.m. — We're not even a mile down the road and I already have to pee.
- 9:10 a.m. — It's unimaginably loud on the bus, which is packed to the gills with kindergartners, first-graders, and a handful of chaperones. I knew I should've brought ear plugs. Even The Animal is dismayed: "How am I gonna live with all this chaotic noise!?" he says. "I mean, I like field trips, but not noisy ones!"
- 9:13 a.m. — The Animal: "This is called the nightmare bus!" Maybe he really is my son after all?

- 9:35 a.m. — OK. My bladder just might explode.
- 9:55 a.m. — Finally we arrive at Consol Energy…er…I mean, PPG Paints Arena.
- 10:04 a.m. — Ahhh. That may have been the longest, most satisfying pee of my life.
- 10:07 a.m. — We settle into our seats and I'm shocked at how cold it is in here. I mean, I know the show's on ice and everything, but do they really have to have the A/C on?
- 10:08 a.m. — I laugh as The Animal asks me to buy him a $15 thing of cotton candy. Funny kid.
- 10:33 a.m. — As the show begins, I pull on my hood to try to conserve heat.
- 10:47 a.m. — I turn to see if my son is enjoying the Disney-princesses-themed show. His blank expression gives me my answer.
- 11:20 a.m.— Thank goodness! The intermission! I make a b-line for the men's room so I can stand under the heated air dryer.
- 11:45 a.m.— I look at my watch. Ugh. Another 45 minutes left!
- 11:53 a.m.— Oooh! A fire-breathing dragon! All right, now we're getting somewhere!
- 11:54 a.m. — And…more princess crap. Yay.
- 12:15 p.m. — The Animal and one of the other boys I'm charged with are obviously not Frozen fans. The third, however, is belting out "Let it Go" like a champ.
- 12:45 p.m. — Hooray! Back on the bus and heading home! Time for a nap.
- 12:47 p.m. — Oh, joy. One of my son's friends wants to play Rock, Paper, Scissors. Fine, but only for a couple of minutes.

- 1:20 p.m. — How many games of Rock, Paper, Scissors can someone play?
- 1:30 p.m. — Finally the kid stops bugging me and goes back to his seat.
- 1:32 p.m. — And now he keeps jumping up from behind the seat to tap my son on the head, which I can tell The Animal clearly enjoys. "He's so annoying," he whispers to me.
- 1:37 p.m. — As the volume once again reaches the ear-splitting level, The Animal yells out: "Worst bus ride of my life!" Like father, like son.
- 1:45 p.m. — Finally we arrive back at the school. I can't wait to run home and take a peaceful, quiet nap before I have to come back and get the kids in an hour. Then the Principal asks me if I'd like to take my kids and my niece home early.

Gee. It's like she read my mind.

Minecraft, Pokémon, and Other Mysteries of the Universe

Of all the great mysteries of the universe — dark matter, black holes, the allure of daytime television, etc. — two in particular have me utterly perplexed: Minecraft and Pokémon.

It all began when my son, aka The Animal, went to school with a $15 Minecraft action figure and then came home instead with four beat-up old Pokémon cards. "I traded with John!" he said excitedly. "Look, Daddy! I got an EX and a Mega EX!" Personally, I thought he got a bum deal. But what do I know?

Before you know it we're buying packs of Pokémon cards at Walgreens (at $5 bucks a pop!) and my son is asking for "tins" of cards ($25 each!) for his birthday and Christmas. Before long those four initial Pokémon cards had multiplied to somewhere around 300 and were scattered all throughout our house, much like those pesky tribbles on the Star Trek Enterprise.

I get the appeal of collecting cards. Heck, I've still got shoeboxes full of old sports cards in the cellar. But unlike those good old-fashioned baseball or football cards, which were for admiring and pretty much nothing else, Pokémon cards are used in a role-play type of game, in which each card can do a different amount of "damage" to those of your opponent. The game itself is sort of like that old card game War, just way more complicated.

The cards are harmless enough. The problem is when The Animal asks me to have a Pokémon battle with him. First of all, he has absolutely no idea what he's doing and pretty much just makes up the rules as we go. He's also a blatant cheater and is constantly stacking the deck pre-deal. We've had tons of battles and not once have I won. (Not that I'd realize it even if I did.) Secretly, I'm OK with that. The way I see it, the sooner I lose, the sooner I can go off and do something more productive with my time.

Like take a nap.

Minecraft is just as frustrating. As video games go, it's downright primitive. I mean, the graphics are terrible. And in a way, I'm offended by it. I didn't slog my way through the rudimentary graphics of the Atari 2600, and then through the so-so imagery of Nintendo and later Sega, just so my own kids would end up playing games with the pixelation of Pong. For cryin' out loud, there are video games out there today that are so lifelike, so realistic, you'd think you were watching a movie. Why on earth would you drive a Pinto when you've got a Ferrari in the garage?

But, hey, for some reason they love it—crappy graphics and all. They'll sit there for hours constructing strange, boxy-looking homes and buildings within a boxy world, while at the same time fending off boxy-looking zombies and boxy-looking giant spiders, all without really accomplishing anything. It's nuts. At least when I was playing my primitive-looking Atari video games there was a purpose: to win the game!

Instead of naming it Minecraft they should have called it Mindless.

But again, what do I know? (Heck, I'm the middle-aged man who's obsessed with Bigfoot.) I guess as you get older, the world of the young just makes less and less sense. Which is fine with me. As they say, ignorance is bliss.

And at this rate it looks like I've got a lot of bliss in my future.

Funny Farm

This past weekend we were fortunate enough to spend some quality family time at a cabin on our friends' farm. The following are the highlights:

Five minutes after arriving on Friday afternoon, The Animal is riding the giant tire swing when he catches his foot on a root, twists his ankle, and screams bloody murder. Not long afterward he's back on the swing when it hits the tree and filthy, stagnant water from within the tire sloshes out all over him.

The next morning while strolling through the surrounding woods, I nearly have a heart attack when I stumble upon a newborn brown calf resting in the leaves. In my defense it could very well have been a baby Bigfoot.

Later on we go to check out the chickens over in the field and the two overly friendly Great Pyrenees roaming the farm slather me with about a gallon of slobber.

That afternoon I chop some firewood I'd purchased at Giant Eagle, somehow managing not to maim myself in the process. I did, however, get a splinter.

Boogs and I spend almost an hour building a super-cool hut out of sticks, which she then plays in for a total of 30 seconds.

That night while getting ready for bed we discover a wolf spider the size of a baseball glove in the bathroom sink. Later on Cass kills another unidentified arachnid just before it crawls on Boogieface's head while she is sleeping. I consider sleeping out in the car but then just decide to drink several beers instead.

Sunday morning as we enjoy our coffee by the fire the kids go off to see the chickens and to their delight discover a squashed and eviscerated frog on the gravel driveway.

Later on we all tramp across the pasture to see the pigs and then watch in horror as one pees for about a minute while the others stick their snouts into the stream and drink it.

Moments later, off in the distance, I spot the dogs eating what I think might be a dead animal. But when I make my way over I realize it's that same calf again just sitting there resting while the big white dogs slurp up its yellow poop like vanilla soft-serve.

Returning to the cabin Boogs hides some "magic crystals" (i.e., plastic lightbulbs) in the surrounding woods and we have a Harry-Potter-themed scavenger hunt, with me playing the boy wizard and my wife his sidekick Hermione.

Meanwhile The Animal decides instead to go off and play with the fire and, much to our surprise, doesn't manage to burn the woods down.

All in all it was a fantastic weekend in the great outdoors. Sure, maybe my Crocs smell like cow manure and I'm filled with shame for being frightened by a baby cow, but it's a small price to pay to see the kids having fun without having to stare at some type of glowing rectangle.

A Sticky Situation

The sound of the bathroom door woke me. I pushed the button on my iPhone: 4:55 a.m. One of the kids must have gotten up to go pee. The light in the hallway followed by a tinkling sound confirmed it. As the toilet flushed and the light went off, I relaxed and prepared to fall blissfully back to sleep. Then a creaking sound and I saw Boogieface silhouetted in the doorway.

I sat up. "What's up, baby? You OK?"

She mumbled something about a "mess" and an "accident." My heart sunk. Nothing's worse than having to get up in the middle of the night to strip your child's bed of urine-soaked bedding and urine-soaked stuffed animals. I take that back: Cleaning up vomit at 3 o'clock in the morning—that's the worst. Been there, done that.

"And it's all in my hair, too." Wait, what? Turns out there had been an accident for sure, but instead of pee it was putty.

You see, earlier that day my daughter had purchased a can of Crazy Aaron's Thinking Putty upstreet at Castle Toys. It was the "Star Dust" kind, which looks like the night sky and glows in the dark. Apparently she had been playing with it in bed and fell asleep. Now she was awake and claiming that her putty was nowhere to be found. Except what was in her hair, that is.

"What do you mean you don't know where it is?" I said. "It has to be in your bed somewhere."

"I don't know. Maybe it fell behind the bed."

Being familiar with my daughter's usual level of effort, or should I say lack of effort, when it comes to doing just about any task, I was certain that the putty was still somewhere in her bed. And as I climbed the steps to her top bunk, my suspicions were confirmed. The putty was still in her bed, all right. Or should I say, all over her bed. The dark, sparkly slime was embedded (ha!) in her comforter, as well as in her favorite "raggie" and a sweatshirt of mine that she likes to sleep with. (For some reason she likes the way Daddy smells. At least one person in this house does.)

So there we were, at 4:55 a.m., digging putty out of my daughter's bedding and hair. My wife was able to get much of the slimy substance out of the comforter, but as for Boogieface's hair, we ended up having to resort to scissors for one big clump of it.

Oh, well. It could've been worse. Putty is a lot more pleasant to deal with than pee or puke in the middle of the night, both of which we have dealt with on numerous occasions. But such is parenting.

Needless to say, playing with putty in bed has now been outlawed in our home. That's another part of parenting, just a way more fun part: spontaneous reactive legislation.

Time to Grin and Bear It

Well, it's official. In the long slog that is parenthood, we've officially entered...The Dental Years.

It all started the other day when the kiddos had their regular six-month check up. So far these have gone pretty smoothly, but of course I knew that wouldn't last. Heck, they eat ice cream every single night, and their nightly teeth-brushing rarely lasts longer than 10, maybe 20 seconds, at most.

So when the dentist told me Boogieface had a cavity, honestly, I wasn't surprised. I did feel bad for her, though. When it comes to cavities, I've been there, done that—about 20 times over. My mouth has more metal in it than a junk yard. The brave little thing, she didn't turn on the waterworks until we got back to the car. Then it was Niagara Falls.

The Animal didn't get off scot free either. No cavities, which was nice. But the dentist did say the boy would need a spacer soon to correct the damage done by his nightly thumb-sucking. Wonderful.

Of course, just as you'd expect from two loving siblings, upon hearing the news of each other's dental disappointment, they immediately took the opportunity to rub it in.

"Now they're gonna stick you with a big needle—in the mouth!" said my son, smiling fiendishly. (The reason he knew about the "big needle" was because I had been telling them both about it in an effort to scare them into brushing better. Fear as a tool—it's Parenting 101.)

"Oh, yeah?" replied my daughter. "Well, you're going to have to brush your teeth AT SCHOOL! So there!"

Yep, when faced with your own failings in life, nothing makes you feel better than bringing others down.

I remember being terrified of the dentist when I was a boy. Not because of anything he did, mind you, but because 99 percent of the time I'd end up having a cavity (or three), and then I'd have to come back in a couple weeks to get a filling. According to my dentist at the time, I had "deep-grooved teeth." Maybe that was the case, but I'm pretty sure my eating habits, like my tendency to eat, in one sitting, an entire bag of Chips Ahoy! cookies dipped in Lipton sweetened iced tea, didn't help. Sometimes I'd just eat the dry iced tea mix right out of the can.

Now we have to decide whether to go the sedation route for Boogsie's filling or let her experience the good old-fashioned trauma of the lidocaine needle and the following hour or two of awkward face numbness. Personally, I think the latter would do more towards influencing her future teeth-brushing thoroughness. Then again, it really didn't do much for me.

We now also have to start the orthodontic journey with my son a little earlier than we had planned. I figured he'd need braces or at least a retainer one day, but I thought we had a good three, maybe four years to prepare for the financial burden.

Oh, well. Such is life when you're a parent. I'm sure we'll figure out something. Maybe I can sell my own fillings for scrap?

Old School Love

I was out and about around lunchtime today, so I decided to swing by my kids' school to see if I could catch them out on the playground.

I got there just as my son's class and the rest of the younger kids were wrapping up their recess. I stood off to the side, trying not to let him see me watching him, while at the same time realizing I looked like some creepy dude spying on the students. I feel like this anytime I am sitting on a local park bench reading while kids are playing on the playground.

The kids in my son's class were playing kickball in a crazy, chaotic manner that only second graders can do. The Animal ran, skipped, and galloped around the bases as his classmates scrambled and fought over the foam-rubber ball bouncing across the black asphalt. Earlier that morning, as we were getting ready to leave for school, we had noticed that his just-one-month-old school shoes were literally falling to pieces. Now I could see why.

I can still remember having recess on that very same parking lot as a student at that school oh-so-many years ago. We were always playing tag or, my personal favorite, keep away. I remember one time in particular, when I was the same age my son is now, and my friend and I were fighting to win the heart of the same girl, the lovely Melissa. Well, the war of worlds got pretty heated between me and one of my classmates, and the next thing you know sensitive 7-year-old Val is off somewhere crying.

Well, my big sister, all 9-years-old of her, took my hand and marched me right back over to my friend and the others who had been picking on me. Then she let'em have it: "Aliens!" she yelled, before leading me away to comfort me.

In the end neither of us won over our beloved Melissa, and my rival and I ended up becoming best friends. Such is life.

I've heard that, so far, my son has no such girl problems, and actually has a few suiters who shamelessly pursue him, much to his (and my) chagrin.

As recess started wrapping up and the kids all got into their respective single-file-lines, my son spotted me and seemed mad that I'd been spying on him. But then, as they passed me to go back into school, he left the line and ran over to see me, making sure that I gave him a hug but, of course, no kiss in front of his classmates.

Well, at least this time I didn't get rejected.

Living with The Animal

Imagine having a goose for a pet. A Canadian goose. But not just any old Canadian goose. A hyperactive, disturbingly loud, never-tired-of-honking Canadian goose.

Now strap a siren to the goose. A siren that never stops wailing, day or night. And make sure it's loud. So loud that it rattles your eardrums no matter how far away in your house you are from the goose.

Next, tie an alarm clock around the goose's neck. One of those cheap alarm clock radios you find in a hotel room. A broken alarm clock that you can't shut off and beeps incessantly. And make sure the volume is all the way up.

Then put some tap shoes on the goose's webbed feet. And while you're at it, stick a few tacks inside each shoe so that the goose will honk loudly with each and every step. And tie a string of empty cans around its body, which the goose will then drag behind it as it follows you around the house.

On second thought, forget the goose.

Too much poop.

Go out and hire a professional yodeler. Preferably a pubescent yodeler whose voice is constantly cracking and sending him way off key. Then give him a megaphone and have him follow you around all day yodeling, at the top of his lungs, the song from the Cliffhangers game on "The Price is Right."

You know what? Forget the yodeler.

Too weird.

Download "The Chicken Dance" song to your smartphone. Now plug in your earbuds, set the song to repeat, and put the volume on high. Start playing it as soon as you wake up and continue playing it all day long until you go to bed.

Now maybe, just maybe, you'll understand what it's like to live with my son, aka The Animal.

And people wonder why I'm always grumpy. (Not to mention hard of hearing.)

Holding On For Dear Life

Recently my daughter, aka Boogieface, turned 10. As I'm sure you can imagine, this threw me into a bit of a panic. We're talking The Big One-O here. Double digits. It won't be long now before that second digit turns into a three and, well, we all know what happens then.

Heaven help me.

So that's why you can understand how ecstatic I was when Boogs decided to spend some of her birthday money on a LEGO race car. A race car! How great is that? After all, in the not-so-distant future she'll be spending her money on things like makeup, skin-tight jeans, or the latest profanity-ladened, disturbingly misogynistic, but really-awesome-to-dance-to hip-hop album.

Just not today. Thank goodness.

I guess you could say I'm hypersensitive about how fast my little girl is growing up. People always told me how quickly time passed when you have kids. Personally, my first eight years of parenthood went by like molasses. Exceptionally thick, slow, painful molasses. It wasn't until my daughter turned eight that I noticed time speeding up.

That's why I was thrilled recently when, upon seeing her brother's brand new Nerf football, my daughter asked me if she could have one of her own. I couldn't drive to the store fast enough. Heck, what's five bucks in the grand scheme of things? In a few years she'll be asking me for the latest iPhone. And when that happens, believe you me, I won't be rushing out to drive to any store.

As Halloween was approaching this year, Boogs was planning on going as "Hermione" from the Harry Potter series, which as far as costumes go nowadays is still pretty innocent. But then at the last minute she decided to go instead as K2SO—the sarcastic yet heroic droid from "Rogue One: A Star Wars Story." Again, I was overjoyed. Let's face it, no girl on the verge of teenagery would be caught dead in some geeky droid costume. But my little girl loved it. And Daddy did too, make no doubt about it.

Look, I know I'm in a losing battle. I can't make time stand still. But as of now we're successfully keeping the dreaded teenage years at bay. My little girl still likes to play with things like LEGOs and Nerf footballs, and she'd still rather dress up like a robot than something more provocative like, say, a sexy bottle of Sriracha. (Yes, that's a real thing.)

Best of all, she still wants Daddy to tuck her in every night. And you better believe this guy is soaking up every last minute of it. Hey, I'm no fool. I know it won't be long before everything changes and she'll want nothing to do with me. Pretty soon she'll be running out the door to hang with her friends or, even worse, some boy-band-lookin', Axe-body-spray-wearin' kid who drives his daddy's Land Rover. Ugh.

Of course, this Daddy will always remain close by. Except then I'll be all decked out in black and sporting a pair of high-powered binoculars.

Like I said, I'm no fool.

About the Author

Valentine J. Brkich is the writer of Small-Town Dad (smalltowndad.com), a blog where he documents his fatherhood misadventures and other humorous aspects of small-town life.

Val's first book, *Cageball, Poker, and the Atomic Wedgie: And Other Tales of Catholic School Mischief*, sold dozens. His ebooks include *Achieving Mediocrity – Surefire Strategies for a Lackluster Life*, and *Get Yourself An Inflatable Baby Sitter – And Other Survival Tips For First-Time Dads*, both of which have helped make Val a household name in his own household.

Val, his wife and their kids – Boogieface and The Animal – live in Beaver, Pa.

ValentineBrkich.com
@valentinebrkich

www.ingramcontent.com/pod-product-compliance
Lightning Source LLC
Chambersburg PA
CBHW071213090426
42736CB00014B/2807